Soul Care

Soul Care

Peter Lord

BAKER BOOK HOUSE
Grand Rapids, Michigan 49516

ISBN: 0-8010-5661-6

Second printing, November 1990

Printed in the United States of America

Scripture quotations not otherwise identified are from the New American
Standard Bible, © The Lockman Foundation 1960, 1962, 1963, 1968, 1971,
1972, 1973, 1975, 1977. Other translations cited are from the King James
Version, The Living Bible, the New Testament in Modern English (Phillips
Edition), the New King James Bible, and Today's English Version (Good News
Bible).

The quotations on pages 49, 67, and 169 are from *Gift from the Sea* by Anne
Morrow Lindbergh. Copyright 1955 by Anne Morrow Lindbergh. Reprinted
by permission of Pantheon Books, a division of Random House, Inc.

The quotation on p. 19 is from *The Search for Significance* by Robert McGee,
© 1985 by Rapha Publishing, Houston, Texas. Used with permission.

The quotations on pages 143 and 203 are from *The Road Less Traveled* by
M. Scott Peck, © 1978 by M. Scott Peck, M.D. Reprinted by permission of
Simon & Schuster, Inc.

The quotation on page 213 is from *Unto Full Stature* by DeVern Fromke, ©
1964 by Sure Foundation. Used with permission.

To
Eli Machen

my son-in-law
friend
minister of God to my soul
a man who has given his life
to soul repair and care
a consultant and helper with this book

Contents

Preface

After being a pastor for forty years, associating with many other pastors, and traveling to many churches across North America, I am convinced that poor soul care has damaged the body of Christ. My dad was a dairyman and if his cows had received the type and quality of care most Christians give their souls, he would soon have gone bankrupt. So it is with us, the body of Christ, the church. The neglect of the developmental process for inner life—soul care—has stunted the growth and potential of many Christians.

God did not intend the church to be a soul hospital but rather a soul spa, a place to develop one's soul to its fullest potential. The church is to be a place where Christians can be conformed to the image of Jesus Christ our Lord.

What This Book Is About

Soul

The way the word *soul* is used in this book is very important. I am a trichotomist, that is, I believe humans are three-part beings: soul, body, spirit. Actually, I have no quarrel with the dichotomist who believes the soul and spirit are one, or equivalent entities. For that reason, I have not sought to differentiate in this book between the terms that most people use to refer to "inner life," and I tend to use the words *soul* and *spirit* interchangeably.

I believe that man does not *have* a soul but *is* a soul with a body and spirit. Through his body, his soul lives and interacts in a physical world, and through his spirit, his soul interacts with the spiritual world.

When Adam and Eve sinned, they not only brought physical death to God's originally perfect creation, but they and their descendants also "died" in spirit. They lost their capacity to commune with God. An unregenerate person is one who is dead in spirit and unable to commune with God.

Jesus, the perfect man, was whole—alive in body and spirit. He could communicate in both the physical and spirit world at the same time. He came to redeem us, to conquer death, and to give us spiritual life.

Care

However, no matter how strong, any potential must be nurtured and developed if it is to become an actual ability. In the physical realm, for example, a newborn may have the capacity to interrelate with the physical world through a sense of hearing. But that capacity must be developed over time if the baby is to understand what is "heard." For every living thing (human and nonhuman) there are specific and special ways to care for it so the inherent potential in that life form may be developed and remain healthy. Dairy farmers have a special way of caring for cows, chicken farmers have a different way of caring for chickens, African violet growers have a definite way of caring for them which differs from the care given to roses.

Soul care has to do with the special things that we do to cooperate with the life God gave to us in the new birth. We want to develop as quickly as possible into our full potential. This developmental process—soul care—is the keynote of this book. The ongoing dynamics involve learning how to actualize the Holy Spirit's empowering so as to grow as quickly and fully as possible into the likeness of Christ. Then we can "be Jesus" for the world and represent him to the glory of God the Father.

Current Character Crisis

The crisis of Christian character in the North American Church has been obvious to me in several ways, the first of which is my personal struggle in living as a Christian. While in my mid-thirties, as a pastor of a successul church ("successful" in the way man usually measures churches—nickels and noses, more and more of them), I arrived at a point of frustration that caused me to write this letter:

> Dear God:
> I believe in you and in Jesus Christ as Lord—but if there is not any more to this than I have discovered thus far, I am quitting at the end of a year.
>
> Peter Lord

I stuck this letter in my desk drawer with a commitment I meant to keep. It was written out of frustration, not with the church, but with my own life:

I was overcome by evil thoughts, lust in particular.

I did not enjoy praying or find it beneficial.

I studied the Bible so I could preach to others, not for my own needs.

I did not truly know God or even know much about him, and what I did know was incorrect.

I was neither experiencing nor practicing what I preached every Sunday.

I was not a deliberate hypocrite. In fact, I was determined not to be one, though I could not grasp the way to change. The Christian life was one constant struggle for me. It was obvious that if something significant did not happen in my faith life, I was headed for trouble. I did not want to disgrace my calling as Christ's ambassador, hurt my family, or ruin my own life, but I saw no way out. So, in desperation, I wrote that letter. And, praise God! he met me at my point of despair. Much of what I share in this book involves the answers he gave me then and is still giving me every day.

A second piece of evidence of widespread "character crisis" in the church is found in the very real struggles most Christians experience. Adding to my personal pain and frustration was my observation that most Christians, including ministers of the gospel, were just like me. When they took off their masks of piety and shed their religious posturing, even for a moment, I could easily recognize them.

I would ask visiting evangelists, "How many triumphant Christians do you know?" Most answered something like "a handful—four, maybe five." There were never more than "a dozen" mentioned. It seemed to me that what we were doing was not working in the way Scripture said it would and in the way it did for a few godly people I knew. Of course, those people—my wife and one or two others—demonstrated in their walk and talk the reachability of a fruitful, overcoming, and joyous Christian life. But there were so very few lives that proved that such reality was possible.

I also began to find negative signs in the facts about most churches. For example, one denominational paper admitted recently to some disturbing statistics, indicating that we cannot find one-third of our people and that another third never attend. This denomination has consistently bragged about being the largest Protestant group in the United States—one that is going to "win the world to Christ" in our generation. We cannot keep our own in the fold, not to mention the sometimes questionable conduct of the third who *do* attend.

Statistics from the denomination with which I am most familiar also show much about the failing spiritual health of its clergy:

1. The number of pastors quitting the ministry (one source made an estimate of three a day).
2. The number of pastors fired by their churches.
3. The great problem of strained relationships that exist between staff ministers. The spiritual leaders of churches cannot get along! One evidence of this is the number of ministers who have a brief stay at one church and then move on to another.

One could go on and on, but suffice it to say that we so-called shepherds are not doing our job of nurturing our flocks and of producing truly Christian believers who act, talk, and walk in an ever-increasing way like Jesus Christ. Something is missing.

The number of pastors who have recently failed in their own lives is another warning sign. As I write this, one of America's well-known Christian evangelists is standing trial for fraud and dishonesty. His moral life has been ridiculed on TV talk shows and in the news media, as is the backsliding of other Christian spokesmen once considered beyond reproach. If I could list the number of prominent people I know who have fallen, it would astound you, as it does me. It is a frightening condition for the church establishment.

Let me make it clear that I could easily be numbered among the "failures" and still might be. The Scriptures that most frighten me on that score are: "They made me caretaker of the vineyards,/But I have not taken care of my own vineyard" (Song of Sol. 1:6b) and ". . . lest possibly, after I have preached to others, I myself should be disqualified" (1 Cor. 9:27b). Let it be clear that I do not stand as judge of others. I ask and pray for mercy and grace both for them and for me.

Finally, we, the professionals, have made the Christian life seem very complex. Look at all the how-to books and tracts adorning the average preacher's bookshelves, material that also finds it way to laypeople in bookstores and conferences. Titles range from *One Hundred Ways to Bind the Devil* to *Seventeen Steps to a Good Prayer Life, Three Hundred Ways to Love Your Children* (or *Your Spouse*), and *Twenty Ways to Build the Hedge of Thorns.*

One day, looking at my own collection, I realized how unreal and futile are such pat formulas. Genuine Christianity must be reachable and meaningful for all people, regardless of their education, material wealth, or past experiences and cultural background. It must work for the engineer at Cape Kennedy who is also a father and husband and for the woman who, as a single parent, must struggle to be both father and mother to her children. Perhaps the most needed message for the church today is found in Paul's words: "But I am afraid, lest as the serpent deceived Eve by his craftiness, your minds should be led astray from the simplicity and purity of devotion to Christ" (2 Cor. 11:3).

For Whom Is This Book Written?

The prescription for the "Christian health crisis" that I attempt to present in this book works in the lives of dynamic Christians who apply it to help them reflect the image of Christ. And it is working day by day in my own Christian walk. *Soul Care* is not written primarily for religious professionals, but for the average, ordinary believer whose heart hungers for the reality of Jesus yet whose mind and spirit struggle to reach that goal. If, dear fellow professional, you think my answers are wrong, write to me and tell me what *you* have found to be the truth. All I have done here is present the light I have received thus far. It is not *all* the light, but it is changing me as I walk in its glow and know the Lord Jesus in a greater and more personal way, loving him more than I ever have before.

How Should This Book Be Read?

I urge you to read this book prayerfully, fully open to the idea of applying these truths to your life. Knowledge can be dangerous unless it is accompanied by appropriate action. It should never become a substitute for love of God and one's fellowman. Love—which Jesus defined as keeping his commandments—edifies and enriches ordinary lives. Most of us know far more about love than we have ever tried to put into practice.

Grace and mercy be with you. I ask that you will pray the same for me.

UNDERSTANDING YOUR SOUL

I am an awesome spirit being
of magnificent worth as a person.
I am deeply loved of God;
I am fully pleasing to God;
I am totally accepted by God.
And when my person
is expressed through my performance,
the reflection is dynamically unique.
There has never been another like me
in the history of mankind,
nor will there ever be.
I am an original,
one of a kind,
really somebody—and so are you!

Robert McGee
The Search for Significance

1

Your Worth

I had stopped to call on Geri, a young mother with a serious alcohol problem. As I walked to the door, the Holy Spirit said to me "Get Geri to talk to me." After exchanging social pleasantries with Geri and her husband, I said, "Geri, God wants you to talk to him." I told her how simply we may hear God and she asked the Father, "Would you please tell me what you think of me." His reply to her was, "You are worth a lot more that you think you are."

I said, "Ask him what you are worth." She did, and then said, "I don't understand the answer. He said, 'Geri, you are worth as much as I am.'"

For a moment I was perplexed too, and then I saw it. Worth is often determined by the price paid for something. Christ gave his life for us so we could have life. Life for life. His life for my life.

What a thought! What a truth! Especially for Geri because she was destroying herself and her family with

alcohol basically because she did not think much of herself. She had a bad self-image, a low self worth. Now a
transformed person, she realizes her worth and no
longer seeks to destroy herself.

When something is valuable to us we take care of it.
We usually don't spend time, effort, or money on something we consider worthless or unimportant. If we understood our real worth we would diligently care for ourselves. Our real worth does not lie in our bodies, they are
just the house we live in. The real selves are our souls.

This is what Jesus was talking about when he asked
the question: "For what will a man be profited, if he
gains the whole world, and forfeits his soul? Or what
will a man give in exchange for his soul?" (Matt. 16:26).
His choice of words contains a startling revelation.

Some versions of the Bible use words implying that
this question refers to a *lost* soul, one devoid of contact
with God and headed for hell. However, the Greek word
used here for "forfeit" is *zemios,* not *appolumi,* which
would be used for "lost sheep" who are alienated from
God and spiritually destitute.

Zemios, on the other hand, is used to indicate "damage." It appears only six times in the Greek New
Testament, including 1 Corinthians 3:15: "If any man's
work is burned up, he shall *suffer loss;* but he himself
shall be saved, yet so as through fire" (italics mine).

Jesus' words, therefore, are indicative not of a soul in
hell, but of a soul in heaven not fully developed, not all
it could be. What he was saying is that if someone were
able to gain the whole world and damaged his soul in
the process, this individual would be the loser. Gaining
the whole world would not be profitable. The logical
conclusion is that we had better accept our soul's value
and pay whatever price is necessary to preserve its
health!

What Is Our Worth?

The worth or value of an object can be measured in at least eight ways. Any one of these ways can make something valuable. But all eight of these are true about every Christian. As you read these may the Holy Spirit help you to see with the eyes of your heart your incredible worth and value as a person to God and then may he give you the desire to care for your soul.

Factors that Determine Worth

1. Who Made It

Worth is often determined by who the maker was, since the identity and qualifications of the creator can give value (or lack of it) to an object.

A painting of a Campbell's soup can would be valuable if Andy Warhol was the artist. Similarly, if Frank Lloyd Wright was a building's architect, that fact alone would give it status. If that outstanding baseball player Willie Mays autographed a game program, the piece of paper would have a high value because of his signature. If it was discovered that Rembrandt painted the picture hanging in your living room, its value would automatically and radically increase. This is true whether or not you like the picture, for its source (who the artist is) determines at least the monetary value of art work.

It was God himself who designed and created your soul! He was your Maker. Your value, in part, is determined by that fact alone. We are valuable because our all-powerful and perfect God made us. The writer of Genesis says: "Then the LORD God formed man of dust from the ground, and breathed into his nostrils the breath of life; and man became a living being [soul]" (Gen. 2:7).

Say this to yourself three times:

I am a person of excellent worth because God, the Creator of all things, is my Maker. He designed me, made me, and gave me life. I am precious, and my soul is extremely valuable.

Why should we make such a confession? First, confession is part of a biblically documented process, an outward expression of an inner happening. Second, truth confessed aloud is reinforced in the soul. The more we hear something, the deeper the impression on our subconscious. Businessmen know this, which explains why you may suddenly find yourself singing an advertising jingle in the shower!

2. What Was Made

Value is also measured by the complexity or magnitude of what the author, artist, or other "creator" made. A book usually has more worth than a greeting card. A mural-sized, full-color painting is more valuable than a small, simple, black-and-white drawing by the same artist. The Air Force Chapel designed by Frank Lloyd Wright would obviously be of more value than a table or chair by the same designer.

God made the universe: the stars and mountains, seas and minerals, trees and animal life. He also made *us*, but our value comes from our nature—what we are:

And God created man in *His own image, in the image of God He created him;* male and female He created them. And God blessed them; and God said to them, "Be fruitful and multiply, and fill the earth, and subdue it; and rule over the fish of the sea and over the birds of the sky, and over every living thing that moves on the earth" (Gen. 1:27–28, italics mine).

This passage is not talking about the physical body (God does not have one). It refers to our true personhood—the soul, or inner man. I am valuable, and so are you, because we are made to be like God. What we are reflects God's image and is immeasurably complex and worthwhile.

Now confess aloud three times:

I am a magnificent person. I am made by Eternal God in his image and likeness. Everything God made is first-rate, but nothing matches my status as a human being, because I am made like him. I am God's eminent, elite, and supreme creation. I and every other human being have the potential for fellowship with him because I am made in his likeness.

3. Uniqueness Scarcity: Supply vs. Demand

Another factor that makes something "valuable" is its scarcity and uniqueness. When something is in short supply, it has value (assuming there is a demand for it!). Gold is more valuable than coal because there is less of it. Diamonds cost more than pearls for the same reason.

Friends in Vancouver, Bob and Joan, gave me two beautiful ceramic ducks that are very valuable, as indicated on a metal plate attached underneath each of them. One of the plates reads:

Widgeon
170/1500
Gosset

The first line is the name of the duck: Widgeon. The third line is the name of the artist: Gosset. But the second line—170/1500—attests to a "limited edition." There will be only 1500 of these made, and this duck is number 170 of that total. If the duck was one of 300,000 stamped out in Taiwan, it would be far less desirable, or valuable, even if the quality *were* the same.

This is why "originals" are so expensive. They are unique, one of a kind. I remember seeing an exhibition of Norman Rockwell originals. The prices were in six figures because each was a one-of-a-kind work by this recognized artist.

Do you know that *you* are an original, too? God has a number on you like the one on the duck. Your number is 1/1. God broke the mold after he made you!

Confess out loud:

> There has never been another like me in the history of mankind, nor will there ever be. I am an original, unique and one of a kind. Really somebody!

Repeat this over and over until it sinks in. A new feeling of self-worth will come to you. Remember that you are the only person who can glorify God in your own special way.

4. Personal Preference and Choice

Things can also be "valuable" to us simply because we like them. Your favorite picture might not be painted by a famous artist. You might find a book worthwhile because its content pleases you (and even though the critics pan it).

"Beauty is in the beholder's eye" means that you like something and value it.

Have you ever realized that God has chosen you? He loves you and wants you in his family. Our man-made version of "Christianity" leaves the impression that we chose God. But genuine Christianity holds that God chose us and called us before we accepted him. In truth, "faith" is *our* acceptance of *his* prior acceptance, our answer to his call and our yielding to his choice of us as his very own.

When God chose us, he knew not only our past but our entire future. Our failures do not surprise him because he knew them beforehand. In fact, he reveals himself to us in these same failures. So each believer can say, "Wow! God chose me because he wants *me*. That makes me very precious to him."

Repeat this often:

I am God's personal choice. He created and then redeemed me because he wanted to. He knew all about me, not only my past, but my future. He chose me, knowing all about me. He saw value in me. He called me and will complete in me what he began. I am of incredible worth to God.

5. Potential Worth

"Potential" refers to hidden riches, waiting to be developed. Many things have value only because of their potential, their possible worth in the future. Suppose you owned a vase that you believed could be worth fifty thousand dollars in ten years, though right now it is "worth" only the fifty dollars you paid for it last week. Would you value and care for it accordingly? Of course you would.

Some people buy stock primarily because of its potential—its "growth factor." Sometimes this works out and sometimes it doesn't, but the point is that stock may be valued because of our estimate of its potential.

Do you know that when you become a Christian you receive all the "spiritual genes" you need to be like Jesus? This means that your soul has the potential, or capacity, to be the image of Christ. Given the proper care, you can become more and more like him every day, which he told us includes fellowshiping with the Father: "If anyone loves Me, he will keep My word; and My Father will love him, and We will come to him, and make Our abode with him" (John 14:23). John reminded us of our great potential: "Beloved, now we are children of God, and it has not appeared as yet what we shall be. We know that, when He appears, we shall be like Him, because we shall see Him just as He is (1 John 3:2).

Potentially, we are like Jesus in the ability to see and hear the spirit world as easily as the physical world, and in the ability to forgive, give, encourage, and walk in holiness and without sin.

To "be Jesus to the world" in character and ability is inherent in every born-again person, as the apostle Paul explained: "For whom He foreknew, He also predestined to become conformed to the image of His Son . . . and whom He predestined, these He also called; and whom He called, these He also justified; and whom He justified, these He also glorified" (Rom. 8:29–30).

You might be asking, "How can I actualize this great potential when I behave and think as I do?" Seeing this potential in yourself is an act of faith. It is faith based on the promises of God and a faith that places great value on your soul.

Say this with me:

> *Seeing the valuable potential in myself is an act of faith. I will not overreact to my wrong behavior and thereby reinforce it. I am able, by God's grace, to see the best in me. By believing the best about myself, I am able to bring out that best. Because God made me, saved me, and indwells me, I have unlimited potential. I am even now a child of God, and I know that when he appears again I shall be like him, for then I shall see him clearly. For now, I accept by faith what he promises. I see my incredible worth as a person, the potential of my soul. This makes me a valuable person who needs to be cared for properly, carefully, and regularly.*

6. Permanence

Suppose you had only one car and knew that it was the only automobile you would ever have. If it were your first, last, and *only* car, would you take better care of it? Of course, you would.

However, we live in a throwaway, replacement society. Since we think of material things as disposable, we transfer this mindset into other areas of our lives. But we must remember that our inner selves are permanent fixtures. You are the only you. Your soul exists not only for today and tomorrow but for eternity.

Death, according to a popular but distorted theology, changes every Christian into a supersaint in heaven. From that view follows the idea that it makes no difference how Christians live here on earth, for death not only eradicates all the evil in them but will transform them into the likeness of Christ.

While I am certainly not an authority in all of this, I know the Scriptures teach that eternity will not be the same for everyone. For one thing, there will be different rewards: "If any man's work which he has built upon it [the foundation of Jesus] remains, he shall receive a reward. . . . If any man destroys the temple of God, God will destroy him, for the temple of God is holy, and that is what you are" (1 Cor. 3:14, 17).

There will be different degrees of maturity, too. An immature soul's experience in heaven will not be the same as a mature soul's. Some will be saved by "the skin of their teeth"—"If any man's work is burned up, he shall suffer loss; but he himself shall be saved, yet so as through fire" (1 Cor. 3:15).

There will be heavenly responsibilities assigned according to an individual's faithfulness on earth. Jesus indicates this in Matthew 25:1, when he begins the parable of the virgins, some wise, some foolish: "Then the kingdom of heaven will be comparable to ten virgins. . . ." Next he tells the parable of the talents and in verse 23 delivers this statement on rewards: "His master said to him, 'Well done, good and faithful slave; you were faithful with a few things, I will put you in charge of many things; enter into the joy of your master.'" Jesus concludes this parable on judgment with a thought that shows how our present life affects us in eternity: "And these will go away into eternal punishment, but the righteous into eternal life" (v. 46).

There lies the bottom line. What we *are*, and *do* here in this life has much to do with what happens in eternity. Death will not bring about replacement of your soul. The "you" represented by that soul is permanent, and there will never be another "you."

Value your soul highly. Care for it wisely. Your inner man is the one lasting thing in the universe that can get better with time if you treat it right.

Say this each morning:

> I am forever. There will not be another me. There can be a changed me, but not a replacement me. God designed me to be forever. In my redeemed state I can choose to be developed or undeveloped, but I will always be me. Part of the intrinsic and high value of my soul is its permanence, its foreverness. So I will take care of the only me I will ever have.

7. Practicality

The more useful something is, the higher its value. Beauty alone may be prized, but when function is added, the worth of any object increases accordingly. So, too, a healthy, maturing soul is not just a pretty picture for the "sweet bye and bye," but has great potential for the "nasty now and now." The real goal of soul care is not to reach an ideal state for some far-off day in heaven, but to enrich our practical living on earth.

If there were no other value in soul care on this side of eternity, it would be worth it not to be sick at heart—to be spiritually healthy. Today, medical experts agree that much illness is "psychosomatic." *Psyche* is the Greek word for soul, and *soma* the Greek word for body. A psychosomatic illness occurs when the body is sick because the soul is malfunctioning.

Besides protecting your general well-being, the fitness level of your soul correlates with what we humans refer to as "happiness." This vague term includes, among other things, the ability to relate intimately with others, the ability to see God in all people and every situation, the ability to be secure and content with where we are, what we have, and who we are.

This is a helpful bedtime confession:

I am remarkable, highly valuable. My life in the body can be fuller and better than I have ever imagined. My health, happiness, and "success" in the overlapping physical and spiritual worlds comprise the practical part of why I must keep my soul healthy, whole, and growing. It is more important to keep myself healthy and whole, than to gain the whole world.

8. The Price Tag

Because of ignorance, blindness, or other factors, we do not always recognize value. But when we find out the price paid for something, we know how valuable it is. For example, except for knowing how to drive, I really don't know much about cars. Traveling on Interstate 95, my son-in-law Eli once commented on a Mercedes that zipped by us: "That car is worth $60,000." I knew it was a valuable car by understanding the price someone paid for it.

Remember the immeasurable price God paid for your soul while you were a non-functioning person (from *his* viewpoint)? You were wrecked, floundering in sinful ways. Yet he purchased you for a great price, not

because you were okay, but because even in your unre-
deemed state he saw an individual of great worth.
Because of divine love, while we were *yet* sinners,
Christ died for us.

If worth is determined by the price paid and Christ
gave his life so we could have life, each individual's soul
is as valuable as his!

His life for my life. What a thought! That truth of
self-worth can set you free. God paid the same price for
you as he did for Billy Graham, James Dobson, Martin
Luther, even Saint Paul. This means that in God's sight
you are as valuable as they are.

What is even more astounding is that God looked at
you, saw your worth, and decided to sacrifice his Son for
your soul's redemption. How can we be aware of that
price tag and not value ourselves?

Confess your worth right now:

> I am a person of great value,
>> of tremendous worth, of high price, of exalted
>> name.
> God loved me and gave his Son for me.
> Christ loved me and gave his life for me.
> Holy Spirit loves me and now lives in me.
>> God is guarding me very closely,
>>> caring for me very carefully.
> I am as valuable to God as any other saint has ever
> been—as valuable as Christ.

An Overview

Any one of the eight factors outlined above determine
your value, but all are true about you. Can you for one
minute doubt your worth?

1. God made you.
2. God made you in his own image.
3. God made you as unique, a one-of-a-kind original.

4. God wanted you, chose you, and called you.
5. You have the potential to be like Jesus.
6. You are a permanent entity.
7. Your soul's health brings practical here-and-now benefits.
8. You were purchased at great price.

I've been a Christian for five years
and God has really worked miracles
in my life. He's "cleaned me up"
in so many ways,
and last week I received
one of his greatest gifts of all—
He convicted me of my righteousness.
For five years
I felt like a dirty, filthy,
sinful, unworthy Christian.
And as I write these words now,
how could those adjectives
ever describe the beautiful,
holy and free life that God gives?
Never! I would much rather feel
like a righteous, awesome, magnificent,
fully loved human being.
And now I do!

A Christian

2

Who Am I?

In his autobiography, *The Ragman's Son*, Kirk Douglas relates this personal experience: "Once while I was driving to Palm Springs, I picked up a hitchhiking sailor. He got in the car, took a look at me and said, 'Hey, do you know who you are?'" Although this was merely the startled response to suddenly recognizing a big star, it is a good question for all of us to ask ourselves.

Do We Know Who and What We Really Are?

On a hot summer day in Florida, three of us were looking for a good used car. Irby Moore is a car expert. John, my son, needed a car, and I was tagging along as any good dad would. We drove from one car lot to another, looking at cars in John's price range. Since Irby was so thorough, our progress was slow, much to my chagrin because it was so hot. He looked at all the inner, hidden things under the hood, especially the engine. John and I were too inexperienced to know where to look or what to look for.

Used-car owners, like most of us, want to make a good impression, so outward appearance is the major emphasis. Externally the cars usually look tiptop, all clean and polished. But Irby knew that such externals do not make an automobile, that it is the internals that enable the car to transport passengers reliably. He knew that a coat of paint can hide many defects. Without an efficient engine, an automobile is useless. The real life and health of a car are hidden underneath the hood. So Irby looked into areas I did not even know existed. Then he started the motor and listened. Next he shifted into gear and actually drove the car. He did all this to determine the real condition of the automobile.

Even though external elements are important, they are not nearly as important as what's inside. The essence of a person is not in such characteristics as facial appearance, bodily build, or clothing. It is the internal and hidden components that make us what we are. Concentration on externals often causes us to miss the more important elements that really make each person unique.

Externals and Internals

Although first impressions seem important in a superficial society like ours, we cannot know what a person is really like by looking at the outside. We easily misjudge others and make basic mistakes in our relationships if what shows is our main measuring tool.

Shakespeare said, "Nature with beauteous wall doth oft clothe in pollution." A modern translation might be:

"Behind a pretty face often lies a devil," or "Appearances can be deceiving."

What the hidden engine is to an automobile, your soul is to your body. It is the real you. Each of us is an everlasting soul with a temporary body, an external chassis. You do not *have* a soul; you *are* a soul. Until you see yourself as a soul with a body, rather than a body with a soul, you will never put the emphasis in the right place.

How a Soul Operates

An engine operates smoothly because its various parts are working well together. A soul is also made of many complex parts, and the condition of these components determines how well the soul (the person) operates.

Soul is the "hidden person of the heart" (1 Peter 3:4a). The word *character* can be defined as "soul," since it usually refers to all the workings of one's inner being. One dictionary defines *character* as "the combination of qualities or traits that distinguishes an individual; personality. The aggregate of features and traits that form the individual nature of some person or thing; moral or ethical quality; qualities of honesty, courage, or the like; integrity; reputation." We might say that "personality" is the projection of a person's soul, while "character" is the actual state of that soul.

Basic attitudes, feelings, and emotions such as anger, love, fear, and lust reside in the soul. These phenomena are part of my soul whether they are right or wrong. Information comes to us by experience, observation, and education, through such channels as newspapers, TV, friends, family, schoolteachers, Sunday school, and church. Our soul stores this information, some of which may be incorrect or harmful. We then operate on this storehouse of data, acting according to what we *believe* is true, whether or not it is true.

A novice can become acquainted with a car's engine when an expert lifts the hood and identifies the component parts: carburetor, air filter, regulator, generator, engine block, fan, fuel pump, radiator, and transmission. All of these are necessary parts in a smooth-working engine. On our car shopping expedition, these were the elements Irby examined and explained.

At this point you may be thinking, *Wait! This is getting too complicated. If I am more complex than a car, I give up. I know so little about my car, and even less about my self—my soul.*

Yes, we are much more complex than a car, but there is a simple solution for us. Just as I sought expert advice when buying a car, we can seek—and find—instructions from our Creator regarding our soul and its health and care.

In the past, my friend Wayne Tucker could repair almost any mechanical problem on a car. Recently he stated that new-model cars are so complex that he can no longer handle many repairs. It takes factory-trained mechanics with computerized sophisticated equipment to do so. Similarly, when we understand how complex we humans are, we will know we can't repair and keep our inner man running well by ourselves.

Our Component Parts

Now let's lift the "hood" to your soul and identify the principal parts that make you the person you are. Your soul is made up of value systems, attitudes, motivations, reasoning plus imagination, conscience, and will (capacity to choose).

Value System

Joe, a junior in high school, spends his time after school working at two jobs. During class he catches up on his sleep. Because he has no time to study, his school work suffers. Why does Joe neglect his studies to hold down two jobs? He is planning to buy a high-performance sports car! Why is he willing to pay such a high price for that car? Because, in *his* value system, a sports car has the highest priority.

Much of our activities and conversation evolves from our value system. The relative worth or importance we assign to different activities and possessions determines how we spend our time, our money, our energies, and our very lives. A car is number one in Joe's value system, so he is willing to make sacrifices for it.

Values—World View

Different world views partially create an individual's value system. One world view holds that all reality is physical and material, that life is limited to the body, and that we cease to exist when we die physically. This view causes people to value physical and material pleasures, even though they are temporary. To them, there is nothing else, since nothing is permanent.

Another world view maintains that the present is primary, so instant gratification is the goal: "You only go around once in life, so grab all the gusto you can." People with this view are not willing to wait or pay the price of long-term effort for results. "I want my pleasure now," they insist.

Others are willing to postpone gratification for a richer, more meaningful life later. Psychiatrist M. Scott Peck, in his best-seller *No Easy Road*, refers to the disciplines necessary to build a fulfilling life. "Delayed gratification" is number one on his list. He defines this as a process of scheduling life's pain and pleasure. We enhance pleasure, he says, by meeting and experiencing the pain first—and getting over it. A young person might express it this way: "Do the tough stuff first so you can enjoy the good stuff to the max." This is why some people are willing to expend time, money, and hard work on college and graduate school so as to enjoy later a fuller life as a professional, whether in medicine, law, engineering, whatever.

A third world view perceives not only the physical, material, and temporal, but the spiritual values of eternity. In this world view the eternal age is more important than the present. Accordingly, individuals holding this view devote adequate attention to their inner selves and timeless values. They recognize the importance of eternal "soul" as well as temporary "body."

Attitudes

Victor Frankl, famed psychiatrist, and former inmate of a Nazi concentration camp declared, "Everything can be taken from man, except the last of the human freedoms, his ability to choose his own attitude in any given set of circumstances, to choose his own way." Frankl underlined the importance of one's attitudes by saying they are untouchable by others. Nobody else can determine or control your attitude toward a given situation.

Let's see the role that attitude plays in soul health. Bill, for example, is a fine person as far as his value system is concerned. He never lies, is dependable, and tends to his inner life as well as he cares for his body. But his general attitude toward life is wrong. Somehow he usually sees the negative, not the positive. He majors on what he does *not* have rather than appreciating what he does have. Thus, Bill focuses on what's wrong with himself, not what's right. He also looks for defects in others and notices corruption rather than "the incorruptible."

See how this negative attitude affects Bill's family.

His teenage son worked two unsolicited hours in the yard one afternoon. When Bill came home from work, he rapidly changed into his grubby clothes and spent the rest of the day working over and criticizing what the son had just completed.

The son remarked, "He never thanked me. He just let me know my work didn't measure up. He's like this all the time. He never sees the cleaned part of the flower beds, only the few straggly weeds I overlooked. Sometimes I just want to quit trying to please him."

Attitudes are part of character—a component of soul. Bill really is a decent person but unpleasant to have around because he is so negative and depressing. He needs an attitude adjustment to have a healthy soul and be a whole person.

Attitude is a key concept for approaching life's challenges. "Every achievement comes from a progression of small achievements. You eat a meal one bite at a time and read a book one page at a time. Your attitude, not your aptitude, determines your altitude" (Lewis R. Timberlake in *Timberlake Monthly*). In other words,

You are what you think.
By filling your mind
with lovely, wholesome,
and uplifting thoughts,
you will find
peace, joy, and fulfillment.

Years ago, when I was at college, my wife and I stayed with a brilliant high-school math teacher. Because he was a dear man of great compassion, he was never harsh in criticism. When asked for an appraisal of another person, he would say only, "He has a good attitude" or "He has a bad attitude." At the time, I considered this a superficial method of assessing people. Thirty-five years later, I am convinced he was right. A person's attitude is one of the fundamental determinants of success, not just in math but in any human task. The rudiments of success are to be found in the mind. It is a principle written in scripture. "For as he thinks within himself, so he is . . ." (Prov. 23:7). The old adage makes the same point.

For instance: No one can live a joyous life if his mind is full of lonely thoughts. What is inside you will always express itself. Think thoughts of loneliness and you will upset your mental well-being and ultimately, your physical well-being. Because your mind is linked to every part of you, it's only natural that when you feel below par mentally you'll start to feel below par physically. That's the definition of "psychosomatic" illness—a manifestation in the body (Greek "psyche").

From *Plus* Magazine

Motivations

Marie has a positive attitude and outlook on life in general and also has a Christlike value system. She does value the truly important matters but so much of the time fear is the basis for her actions, her driving force. She worries about the future (and also about her past "mistakes"). She fears what other people will think, so she is continually anxious that she will be misunderstood. And so on!

Marie's values are right, her attitudes are good, but her motives need adjustment. A fearful approach to life will sooner or later damage one's internal soul engine. God built us to run by love, not fear. If we run with everything not working properly, we eventually damage ourselves and others. That is why positive motivations (the underlying reasons we do what we do) are needed if a soul is to be healthy and full-functioning.

Imagination

Imagination is the soul's ability to put your mind—your "reasoning" component—in places and situations where you are not physically present. We might say, "Oh, I'm sorry. My mind is a million miles away."

Some Christians belittle and condemn imagination as self-indulgent or "unspiritual." Sure, there is an improper use of imagination—vain and covetous daydreaming—but there is a right kind of imagination, too, the kind that is directed toward God and his purposes.

In *My Utmost for His Highest*, Oswald Chambers writes:

> Is your imagination stayed on God or is it starved? The starvation of the imagination is one of the most fruitful sources of exhaustion and sapping in a worker's life. If you have never used your imagination to put yourself before God, begin to do it now. It is no use waiting for God to come; you must put your imagination away from the face of idols and look unto Him and be saved. Imagination is the greatest gift God has given us, and it ought to be devoted entirely to Him.

Every designer, artist, or musician sees something special with his mind's eye in order to create a new reality. Is this wrong? Or is it wrong for a husband to use his imagination in planning a surprise birthday party for his wife? Of course not.

Our lives would be so empty without imagination, and we use it so often that we are unaware of its power and presence in our behavior. Using imagination is especially critical for the Christian because of the part it plays in one's faith life.

Through God's empowerment, in his imagination Noah saw a boat *before* he built it, Abraham saw the Promised Land *before* he arrived there, and Joshua saw Jericho's walls falling *before* they collapsed.

God said that young men shall see visions, and old men shall dream dreams. Where does this take place? In the imagination—the eye of the soul.

Will

My will is to my soul what the transmission and steering mechanism are to a car. The transmission sends the power of an engine to the wheels, which then move forward (or in reverse). The steering mechanism fine-tunes the direction of movement. My will transmits the power of my soul to my body and determines the direction of the resulting activity.

Suppose I have a desire (motivation) to minister to a friend and know (imagine) exactly how I can do this effectively. Nothing actually happens until my will orders my hands and feet to get up and get busy. Almost everything I do with my body is subject to my will.

Will: Our Most God-like Quality

When God made us in his own image, he gave us the right to choose. He could have created us robotic. Robots do not have a choice as to whether they will run. Mechanical inventions work at the will of another. But God has given us the eternal right to choose our actions. He does not and will not force us to do anything.

Yes, we can have habits that bind us in either a good or bad way, but these habits are a result of repeatedly making certain choices. This consistency makes it easier and easier to "choose," often with no conscious exertion of our will. Our lives reflect a series of habit patterns that we have developed or are in the process of developing. To change our lives, we must change our habit patterns. To do that, we must decide to have our motivation, attitudes, and values adjusted.

Even when our behavior patterns are commendable, we must choose to maintain the attitudes, motivation, and values that produced them. In facing daily pressures, if we neglect solid habit patterns, they will deteriorate. We have all seen people change for the worse because they did not make the choices necessary for proper soul maintenance!

Other Functions of the Soul

Soul is the place where I remember, recalling what I have learned in the past, whether true or false. It is also where I put facts together and arrive at certain conclusions.

Soul is also the place where I continually receive new information—where I compare it with what I already have or automatically file it away. Here, too, both virtues and vices are developed and strengthened until they become etched upon our character portrait. It follows that soul is the place where peace or worry resides, where joy or unhappiness abounds, where faith or unbelief springs forth, and where love or hate reigns supreme.

The Bible makes several statements about the soul, especially the part it calls the heart:

"My soul waits in silence for God only . . ." (Ps. 62:1).

"'And do not fear those who kill the body, but are unable to kill the soul . . .'" (Matt. 10:28).

"Watch over your heart with all diligence, For from it flow the springs of life" (Prov. 4:23).

"A tranquil heart is life to the body . . ." (Prov. 14:30).

". . . For the mouth speaks out of that which fills the heart" (Matt. 12:34).

Reputation vs. Character

At Sea World, audiences are entertained by seals trained to act like people. Why do the seals act that way? To get a reward—food. But you can be sure that when they go backstage, they act like seals again.

An actor is a person playing a part, which might be one completely different from what he or she is really like. Actors have to consciously change their natural selves. They cannot be spontaneous.

The Bible labels religious actors "hypocrites," people who outwardly portray something they are not on the inside. They are only role playing. God is not interested in actors, but in real people who live spontaneously and honestly.

In public hypocrites are playing parts for rewards from other people, but when they get offstage and go home, they become their real selves. Someone said that "reputation" is what your neighbors *think* you are, and "character" is what your family *knows* you are. A truly honest person will always be honest, even when he or she can be dishonest and not get caught. This is how good character operates—in the soul, the place God looks, cares about, judges, and examines. Soul *is* you: the real person. What is the real you?

That will be discussed in the next chapter.

Perhaps one can shed . . . one's pride,
one's false ambitions,
one's masks, and armor.
Was that armor not put on
to protect oneself
from a competitive world?
If one ceases to compete,
one does not need it?
Perhaps one can at last in middle-age,
if not earlier,
be completely oneself.
And what a liberation
that would be!

Anne Morrow Lindbergh
Gift from the Sea

3

A Bundle of Contradictions

Okay—the real me is not my body but my soul, the inner and hidden me. But I have a problem. Many of my thoughts, feelings, ambitions, desires, and ideas are often contradictory.

Sometimes it seems a part of me wants to hate, and another wishes to love.

One part of me yearns to trust, yet unbelief and doubt fill another part of my being.

A part of me likes to serve others, and another part is selfish.

A part of me desires God, but there's another part that does not.

A part of me wants to quit, and another part chooses to go on and try again.

A part of me itches to grow and improve, while another part doesn't care whether or not I change.

So which is the real me?

New Creations

Scripture declares that ". . . if any man is in Christ, he is a new creature; the old things passed away; behold, new things have come" (2 Cor. 5:17).

A Christian is a new creation with new quality of life—a new species of being, a child of God given God's nature.

If I am a new creation, what about all these contradictory thoughts? Where do they come from? Am I two persons, one-half good and one-half evil? Part godly and part satanic?

If there were an animal one-half dog and one-half cat, it would be perfectly natural for it to act like either a dog or a cat. It would bark some of the time and meow the rest. Similarly, if I am one-half saint and one-half sinner, am I not reflecting what I am? How can I be held responsible for my actions?

The difference lies in our creation in God's image, including the capacity to *choose* our actions. We Christians are not expected to sin, but when and if we do, God makes provision for us. Scripture teaches that if we sin, we have an Advocate. Am I one-half a new creation and one-half sinner? No, I am a brand-new creation in Christ Jesus. As I strive to attain the maturity he represents, I sometimes sin, but the contradictory me is not the real me. The sinner in me is attached to what I really am, a child of God.

The Kudzu Vines of Georgia

In central Georgia and other parts of the South, a common sight is trees completely covered with kudzu vines. Often these lush-green leafy vines completely hide the tree and even small houses.

Although imported to be a ground cover to combat erosion, these vines are now a curse. Covering acres and acres of excellent timber and farmland, they slowly destroy other vegetation. And the kudzu begins as a little seed but is almost impossible to eliminate, once it sets its woody roots.

Spiritual and moral kudzu vines choke our world and hide our true identity. They begin as insignificant seeds of thought and grow into massive systems of destructive thinking, completely distorting and hiding our real nature, even from ourselves. Jesus warned in a parable about weeds that choke the true plant and keep it from bearing fruit. The kudzu vine is not really the tree whose exterior it covers. It is a foreign element, so attached to the tree that one could easily mistake it for the tree itself.

The Giant Yopang Trees of Borneo

This description from *Jennie and the Song of the Meadowlark* (Robert Bryant Mitchell, Des Moines, Open Bible Publishers, 1988), is an example of the takeover of one organism by another:

> Never had we seen such a tangle of vine and tree. So covered with parasites were these great giants of the forest that it was difficult to decide which was the original trunk.
>
> These creepers simply wriggle their way up the trees exactly like a serpent. It is impossible to pull them off without tearing the bark because thousands of tiny claws have embedded themselves in the tree.
>
> These parasites sap the very life out of the tree, and here and there you see the remains—great, gaunt skeletons standing against the blue sky, every leaf gone; all smaller branches gone, and the creepers now gone also. The tree is dead, wrecked . . . a monument to the work of destroyers . . . the smaller has killed the mightier.

So also do *we* allow worldly parasitical organisms to grow upon our new beings, entwining themselves with our souls until they appear to be a legitimate part of us. This causes our confusion about which is the real me. The narrator continues:

> Yes, there are men, noble men, godly men made in the image of the Creator for His glory, but who are also smothered, defeated, wrecked, arms hanging helpless.
>
> How? Satan, the tormentor, the oppressor and depressor, has used every device to sap the strength. . . . This archenemy knows the weak spot in every life, and it is there he puts in his tentacles—oppressions, imaginations, disappointments, physical weaknesses, moral weaknesses, discouragements—to sap the life, both physical and spiritual.
>
> I know another stately tree, the Cedar of Lebanon, that, instead of nourishing parasites, kills them. The life within is so strong and robust that, instead of feeding the parasites, it chokes them off.

Let us discover how we can be Cedars of Lebanon, mighty souls who destroy and overcome the parasitical forces that disguise our beings, rather than allowing ourselves to be "smothered and defeated." We must learn how to release God's spirit within us, but first we must face a few realities about ourselves and deal with them.

Germ Warfare

Diseases are caused by hostile germs in our bloodstream. They affect us with their poisons in various ways, but these germs are not a real part of us. They are a foreign invasion bent on destroying us. They are *in* me but are not *of* me.

The apostle Paul describes the struggle even this godly man had in his inner being: "But if I do the very thing I do not wish to do [that which is contrary to holy Law] . . . no longer am I the one doing it, but sin which indwells me" (Rom. 7:16–17).

Even as germs corrupt us physically, so sin with all its tentacles attacks the inner man. When these corrupting forces have been there for any length of time, we begin to accept them as part of us. Once we are in this state, it is impossible to rid ourselves of these parasites without considerable pain.

Masks and Disguises

Another way to understand this contradiction about our real selves is to see the masks we wear. We wear these disguises for protection because we have not followed through and dealt with our inner weaknesses and faults. Most of us have never discovered the real persons we are.

In his book *Seeds of Greatness* (Revell, 1983), Denis Waitley deals with mask wearing:

> Don't be fooled by me. Don't be fooled by the face I wear. I wear a mask. I wear a thousand masks—masks that I am afraid to take off; and none of them are me.
>
> Pretending is an art that is second nature to me, but don't be fooled. . . . I give the impression that I am secure, that all is sunny and unruffled within me as well as without. . . . But don't believe me, please. My surface may seem smooth, but my surface is my mask. . . .
>
> Beneath lies no smugness, no complacence. Beneath dwells the real me in confusion, in fear, in aloneness. But I hide that. . . . I panic at the thought of my weakness and fear being exposed. That's why I frantically create a mask to hide behind—a nonchalant, sophisticated facade—to help me pretend, to shield me from the glance that knows. But such a glance is precisely my salvation . . . . if it's followed by acceptance; if it's followed by love. . . .
>
> Who am I, you may wonder. I am right in front of you. Please . . . love me.

A Closet Full of Masks

We all have a closet full of masks, one for every situation, we hope. When we don't have a mask, we are very uncomfortable and insecure. If we get caught with the wrong disguise, we are terribly embarrassed. These masks are our costumes and disguises—talk, body posture, facial expressions—the garments we put on for the different occasions in life. We think these masks make us acceptable to others because they help us appear to be something we are not but wish we were.

Traveling and ministering in many different streams of Christianity, I know exactly which masks to wear to be accepted and thought of as one of "us" by each group. That includes knowing the proper religious phrases to use—the work and experience of the Holy Spirit, for example. You had better refer to him in the right way! One group praises "the baptism of the Spirit," while another group puts this concept down. With some groups, lifting your hands is mandatory. Others do not allow this at all. In some circles it is best not to even mention the Holy Spirit. It doesn't take you long to learn which expressions to use with a given group.

Of course, sometimes you get caught in situations where you have to switch masks very quickly or you may be caught without a mask (or with the wrong one). Somehow our overdeveloped theology does not allow us to be honest and open.

Real believers, it is simplistically stated, cannot have low times, down times, hard times, and be in "right fellowship" with God. So different groups have developed different ways of dealing with the reality that life is difficult at times, that everyone experiences events that get them down. One group will say that if you had faith enough, you would not be feeling low. Another group will encourage you to "choose" different emotions such as happiness and peace. We're taught to deny our feelings, so when the church usher asks, "How are things with you?" we answer, "Fine!" regardless of how we feel.

Why We Wear Masks

We wear masks for many reasons. Some of us have been trained since childhood to do so. We were told, "If you do that or say this, people won't like you," so we soon learn that to be accepted and approved by others we must wear these protective coverings. Another reason we wear masks is that many of us really do not like ourselves, and we fear that if others knew us as we really are, they would not like us either.

The Damage

We seldom assess or think about the damage caused by wearing masks. When we understand the injury that wearing masks inflicts on us, we will be more willing to pay the price to take them off.

Masks keep God out. We can never have a right relationship with God as long as we wear masks when relating to others. God will not rip off our pretentious masks. He waits patiently for us to get honest and remove our own masks, although he does respond to our honest cries for help. He waits for us to become vulnerable and open. Then he strengthens us. One of the reasons we find the Psalms so meaningful is because the psalmist freely and honestly expresses all his feelings to God. For example:

> Remember, O LORD, against the
>   sons of Edom
> The day of Jerusalem,
> Who said, "Raze it, raze it,

> To its very foundation."
> O daughter of Babylon, you
>   devastated one,
> How blessed will be the one who
>   repays you
> With the recompense with which
>   you have repaid us.
> *How blessed will be the one who*
> *seizes and dashes your little*
> *ones against the rock.*
>   (Ps. 137:7–9, italics mine)

The vehemence in this psalm is an honest expression of the psalmist's heart. Yet God did not punish him for such evil thoughts.

We mistakenly believe that God doesn't like us when we indulge in bad thoughts or actions. So we pretend to be better than we are, forgetting that God knows all about us, that he hates hypocrisy and does not respond to pretension.

Masks Not Needed

Our salvation is based on the truth that God loves us unconditionally and bids us to come, just as we are:

> For we do not have a high priest who cannot sympathize with our weaknesses, but one who has been tempted in all things as we are, yet without sin. Let us therefore draw near with confidence to the throne of grace, that we may receive mercy and may find grace to help in time of need (Heb. 4:15–16).

Who needs mercy and grace? Those who have "blown it" and acknowledge their failings. God does not say, "Get cleaned up and then come to me." He says, "Come, and I will help you cleanse yourself."

If you want fellowship with God, take off your masks,

just as Paul says: "But we all, with unveiled [unmasked] face beholding as in a mirror the glory of the Lord, are being transformed into the same image from glory to glory, just as from the Lord, the Spirit" (2 Cor. 3:18).

Masks and People

Masks keep other people out. When we wear masks, we have shallow and superficial human relationships. Yet we all need deep and meaningful relationships, those that bring love and help to enrich our lives.

Meaningful relationships are those where we can be ourselves, where we can share our faith and doubts, our love and fears, our joys and sorrows, our strength and weakness—where we are accepted with all our scars and deformities and are loved and cared for. Masks keep people out of our lives, yet we *need* people.

Masks ensure that defective traits will not be healed. It has been my experience that the quickest way to be healed is to bring my wounds and needs to light—to unmask them—to admit to myself (God and others) that I have hurts that need healing and problems that need to be solved. Evil thrives in darkness. It cannot be eradicated as long as it is unrecognized, but it is part of the nature of evil to stay hidden. This is why confession is such an important part of recovery.

The pure and undefiled gospel of grace says we are welcome into God's presence just as we are, with all our faults and hurts and needs. All we need do, like little children, is to crawl into his lap and ask for help.

Masks make us careful pretenders. Masks are pretentious. Behind our masks lurk our insecurities, and we constantly live in fear of the disguise slipping and our real selves being exposed. Life becomes one big act, one role after another, as we desperately try to be accepted and liked—not for who we are behind the mask, but for who we think everyone else wants us to be.

Without Wax Masks

Especially in the days before photography, sculpturing was a popular artistic profession. Individuals would commission sculptors to do a particular work, and these patrons usually set high standards for the finished product.

Then, as now, there were craftsmen who tried to do authentic and superior work and others who were "just making a living." Of course, all craftsmen make mistakes, but some seek to cover up their mistakes and pretend their work is perfect.

There were once sculptors who learned to cover up their errors with wax that matched the marble they carved. Many were so good at this that it took a trained person to know when there was no wax in the piece of art. So genuine and sincere craftsmen working on a piece of art would hire inspectors to examine their work for wax. After examining the work, if it was found to be error-free, the inspector would declare that it was *sine cera* ("without wax")—the real thing.

Masks are like wax used to cover up what we believe to be our faults and errors. They give a false impression to others about what we are. God wants people *sine cera*, people who are real. You and I are the same way. We want to relate to people who are without pretense and coverup.

Result of Wearing Masks

Masks make us shallow people. Masks affect the openness of the soul so that its maturation and development become retarded. When this happens, an individual can have a twenty-five-year-old body and the emotions of a twelve-year-old.

Have you ever met a so-called adult with a child's emotions and personality? Such people are everywhere. Adult men shirk their responsibilities, even destroy their homes, because they want the freedom to "be young again." Adult women spend their lives in slavery to the latest fashion fads or addicted to the unreal values of soap-opera fantasies.

Masks cause us to live on the surface. Even in solitude, we're not free to get down into the soul, the inner self and find the motives and attitudes that lie there, those that could help form our character into the potential we have in Christ. Masks block off the soul's capacity for intimacy and open communication, for personhood.

Hating to be quietly alone, we prefer noise. We keep busy so we have no chance to get close to ourselves. I am persuaded that the inner tension between what we really are and what we want to present to others is the cause of countless physical illnesses. The body cannot live in mental and emotional conflict without responding to it negatively.

Deceptive Packaging

Masks keep us from correcting the problems that affect relationships with God, self, and others. This self-imposed wrapping damages us because we become confused about our identities. The imaginary me becomes such an effective disguise that it hides the real me from others and myself. Then I may treat the masked me as real. For instance, if evil thoughts run through my mind I might become convinced that they come from the real me—that *I* am evil—when in reality they are darts from the enemy. How do I take care of this confusion?

Recently in a grocery store I saw one of our church members reading the fine print on a box of cereal. She was checking the ingredients in the package because she wanted to know exactly what her family would be eating.

Through its laws, our country declares it a crime to lie about the contents in a box of cereal. These laws demand that the outside of the package tell the truth about what is on the inside. Deceptive packaging is illegal. "Truth in advertising" regulations are another way to protect the public. A good example of this is the warning on a pack of cigarettes: Smoking causes lung cancer, heart disease, emphysema, and may complicate pregnancy."

Unfortunately, there are no such laws about people. We require no one to tell what really lies behind the packaging—the clothes, facial expressions, mannerisms, speech patterns, or affected behavior. No one is forced to tell you what he or she is really feeling, thinking, or planning to do.

Our deceptive packaging—the way we appear to others—is an accepted, even an expected, part of our way of life. We have become experts in this type of trickery. Before we are going to get the help we need, we need to confess this sin of hypocrisy. Only then can we go on the path of discovering and knowing our real selves.

Discovering the Real You

Soul care begins with discovering the real you. How can you discover who and what you really are? How can you discern the unique you whom God knows, sees, and loves? Here are a few suggestions:

1. *You can believe what God says about you.* There

are at least three opinions about you as a person—God's, others' (could be many of these), your opinion of yourself. Which one of these is "true," or accurate? God's opinion, of course. So you need to find out what God thinks about you, by hearing what he says you are.

Carefully reading the New Testament, you find that God uses dozens and dozens of expressions to describe Christians. Not one of them is negative. Here are a few: beloved children, saints, chosen people, royal priests, people of God, his inheritance, sons and daughters. Until you have accepted God's evaluation of yourself, you will keep on believing that the masks *are* you. Believe what God says about you. This is the foundation to discovering who you really are.

2. *Discover the real expression of yourself in your most intimate relationships.* I have often said to my congregation, "The real Peter Lord is not completely known in the pulpit. If you want to know what I'm like, ask my wife." We choose to be what we really are with people who accept us and make us feel secure. Then we do not feel the basic need to wear masks.

I know my wife is committed to me. She will not be turned off by the real me. I know she accepts me as I am, so I can *be* me. The same principle works in true friendships.

Similarly, an employer can afford to be natural because he is secure in his position as company head, but an employee often wears masks because he is afraid of losing his job.

3. *The real you is likely to show up when there are no fences.* Many of the men in our church travel because of their jobs in the space program. I tell them that what they do on the road—the movies they attend, the TV they watch in motel rooms, the magazines they read in private, and the places they go when they are

unknown—are good indications of the true condition of their inner selves.

You can know what you are really like when there are no fences or restrictions to hold you in: limited finances, peer pressure, legal restraints. For example, many people I know, if given enough money to be financially secure, would make drastic changes in their lifestyles. The changes *you* would make in that situation are indications of the desires and goals of the true self within you.

4. *Scripture gives us ways to see our inner selves.* First take the *Treasure Test* (Matt. 6:21—"'. . . where your treasure is, there will your heart be also'").

If you are honest, your treasure shows your heart's true value system: your ideas about what is worthwhile, the things you think important, where you rank your treasures of time, attention, and money. That explains why a man more interested in watching his favorite TV program than helping his child with a school project is only fooling himself when he tells someone how deeply he loves his child. And if he spends more time with his hobbies and recreational pursuits than with his wife, he is showing where his heart really is.

A woman who prefers spending hours in the shopping mall, or watching the daily soap operas, to facing the reality of her family's needs shows where her soul is, no matter how loudly she sings in the choir.

Next take the *Think Test* (Prov. 23:7—"For as he thinks within himself, so he is"). Your frequent and regular daydreams will show you your heart. Because no one (but God) can see your dreams, your imaginings, your desires, and your fantasies, you are free to imagine what you want. But the real you shows up, good or bad. For example, a mother, though confined to home with three small children, visualizes helping an elderly widow five miles away. This reveals the kind of person she really is, not her actual performance while "fenced in" by her responsibilities as a wife and mother.

Finally, take the *Talk Test* (Matt. 12:34b—"'For out of the overflow of the heart, the mouth speaks'"). Jesus is saying that what your heart is full of, your mouth will *easily* talk about. Over and over again, your words will reveal your heart. What does your conversation say about you? Is what you say muffled or distorted by a mask? Or are your words allowed to flow freely from a heart tuned to God's purposes?

How to remain whole
in the midst of the distractions of life;
how to remain balanced,
no matter what centrifugal forces
tend to pull one off center;
how to remain strong,
no matter what shocks
come in at the periphery
and tend to crash the hub
of the wheel. . . .
Perhaps a first step,
is in the simplification of life,
in cutting out some of the distractions.

Anne Morrow Lindbergh
Gift from the Sea

4

Maintenance Principles

Look at that car! Perfectly clean, polished like new. Not a scratch anywhere—and the engine purrs like a healthy kitten. Harry, a high-school junior owns that car. He knows every word in its maintenance manual! Listen as he shows you his car and talks about its merits. You know that it is his special treasure, a matter of great importance to him.

Now look at Harry's bedroom—it looks like gale force winds hit it. What about his last report card?—C's and D's and one F. Now listen to the way he speaks to his parents—at best it is a strained relationship.

Why such a difference in his behavior?

Harry values his car and gives it diligent watchcare. His bedroom, his grades, and his family relationships are unimportant to him, so he does not give them proper attention.

It is easy to distinguish what we value and thus care

for in the external world. Cared-for hair is neat, clean, and attractive. Cared-for lawns are green, trimmed, and weed-free. Cared-for homes are painted and clean, their appliances well-functioning.

When we value anything, we find out how to take care of it and then take the time to apply what we have learned. For example, in the Western World in recent years there has been a new emphasis on body care. The deteriorating condition of our physical bodies, brought on by our prosperity and availability of leisure time, has caused this attention to body fitness. Countless TV programs, videos, books, and health centers exist to instruct and motivate us toward proper physical care. But all the instruction in the world will not change your behavior if you don't value your body. The same idea applies to "soul maintenance."

Why So Little Soul Care?

One word—ignorance—sums up *why* we do not care for our souls, why we neglect the "owner's manual."

Do you know many people who are aware that they are a soul within a body? How many people talk about the condition of their inner life? How many are concerned and spurred to action by the condition of their soul?

Listen to the requests that are shared at the next prayer meeting you attend. How many of them are petitions for soul improvement and how many pertain to physical and material needs? You will find that about 90 percent of these requests are for the latter.

If we are not conscious of something, we don't treat it properly. All drivers know that a car *has* an engine, but few think "engine" when they think "car." Obviously, though, a car is only as good as its engine, the "soul" of any automobile. Some drivers refer to color, body style, and comfort when they think "car." The only time they worry about the engine is when it will not start or run properly. By then they have a crisis, disabling not only the car, but their bank account as well.

If you have read this far, you are probably convinced that your soul exists. Doesn't it make sense to maintain it properly? Only frequent tune-ups will keep it running smoothly.

Even when conscious that there *is* a soul, many people assume that a soul takes care of itself. So they practice benign neglect. They believe that soul is like a tree in the forest, needing no treatment other than what nature provides. They notice the need for soul care only in a time of crisis. Usually, they try to meet the crisis and then neglect the soul till another major problem comes along.

Do you grasp that all of life is dependent upon and in direct relationship to the health and maturity of your soul? I hope so, for ignorance about the need for soul care can result in disaster. To conclude that a soul stays healthy, except in cases of deep calamity, is based on a false assumption, one that leads an individual to major on cure, never on prevention.

Many individuals seek help from pastors, counselors, and psychiatrists when they need advice about a dreadful situation in their personal or professional lives. But if there have been years of neglect to the needs of the soul, the damage has been done, and they face an unnecessarily long road to recovery.

Prevention Is the Name of the Game

The church has fallen into the same trap that has ensnared much of the medical profession. The emphasis

72Understanding Your Soul

is on curing, not preventing, a problem. Until recently, the average medical-school training barely mentioned nutrition and exercise, the basics of any sound health program.

Let's try an analogy—a "parable for pastors." A certain rancher has a pasture for his large herd of cattle. On one end of the pasture is a steep cliff. The pasture has not been well tended, so the grass is dead in most places. Looking for good grass, the cattle wander aimlessly. Because the fence is down, some of them fall off the cliff in their search for food.

Where is the rancher in all of this? Why is he not restoring the pastures for good grazing and repairing the fences to protect his cattle? He is too busy at the foot of the cliff, taking care of the cattle that have tumbled off and hoping to save some of them. These are the emergency cases. He has also spent a lot of time chasing strays that have wandered into the wilderness (where they are easy prey for predators) or onto the neighboring ranchers' pastureland.

Added to this is his continual preoccupation with the science of animal husbandry and his attendance at seminars on cattle care, so as to keep up with the latest methods. He has *no time* to build fences at the top of the cliff or restore the pastures.

This little scenario gives you a good idea of what the average preacher does and why the church is in the shape that it is in today! The typical pastor preaches on Sunday and runs an ambulance service at the bottom of the cliff during the week. Monday through Saturday, church leaders take care of the real crises, those needing immediate attention. The emergencies take a pastor's mind off the need to build fences at the top of the cliff. Most of his (or her) time and energy is spent on repair work and preparing the Sunday message. He has been taught that a powerful sermon is the best way to keep people from running off the cliff, but true crisis prevention is not part of most pastor's training.

As a pastor, I have often felt like a lifeguard supervising hundreds of people in the pool at the same time. I am so busy pulling people to safety after they get into trouble in deep water that I do not have time to teach them how to swim.

Due to lack of proper instruction, some people give up swimming forever. Some people timidly hang around the pool but never dive in. Some do take the plunge but have to be pulled out over and over again. Some drown.

Top-of-the-Line Living

Where do you live?
place of excellence
place of safety
get by
no longer getting by
crisis situation

Are you just "getting by" in life, whether physically, financially, or in your relationships? If so, you are neglecting your soul's health care.

"Get by" living is always one step away from crisis. The slightest slip or change in circumstances will hurl you into disaster. Frequently, people who "just get by" do not seek help to determine why things go wrong and how to correct their behavior patterns so as to prevent future trouble. They simply want relief from their present pain. They try temporary Band-Aid adjustments, when in reality the inner man—the soul—must be painstakingly restored and rehabilitated.

This kind of on-the-edge lifestyle mistreats your soul, which can be compared to running an engine without oil until the engine freezes up. We can't repair a frozen engine by simply adding oil. It must be taken apart and rebuilt, replacing the damaged parts.

Doesn't it make more sense to live at what I call "the line of excellence"? This means doing everything according to the highest standards, by conviction and principle, aiming for excellence in every area of life. When such a person has a setback and falls a little, he does not fall into disaster.

Even in a "crisis," his soul can repair itself and continue to aim for "the best."

Everybody slips and falls or has setbacks in external circumstances. Storms hit us all, and if we are just getting by (living on the edge of a crisis), these storms will submerge us in deep water. This is very easy to see in the area of finances, but it is equally true in the realm of the soul. If we place ourselves at the excellence level, setbacks will not be so disastrous. Our souls flourish in a top-of-the-line approach to life.

Nutrition and Exercise for the Soul

Healthy bodies are not an accident but the result of definite maintenance procedures. A formula for good physical health would look like this:

Good Food
+ Right Exercise
+ Proper Rest
+ Right Thinking
= A Healthy Body

Poor physical health in America, the richest country in the world in terms of natural resources, is not due to *what* we have, but *how* we use it. In this land of plenty, we violate the basic laws of good health.

Experts find that eating junk food, lack of exercise, worry, fearful thinking, and stress are contributing causes to our poor health. Fortunately, out of these discoveries has come a renewed emphasis of the ways to good health, including an abundance of fitness centers, health-food stores, hundreds of books on proper diet, the President's Council on Physical Fitness, warnings about such things as inferior diet, cholesterol, and carcinogenic food.

But there is still an abysmal ignorance about the care and feeding of the soul. Try this questionnaire:

---

1. What is soul food?

_____

2. What are three good soul foods?

_____   _____   _____

3. List three bad soul foods.

_____   _____   _____

4. List the items in your soul-care program—the planned activities you do to care for your soul on a regular basis.

_____

_____

_____

_____

_____

_____

5. If a new Christian asked you, "I want to grow in the quickest possible way into the likeness of Jesus Christ, do you have any advice for me?" what would you say?

_____

_____

_____

Mere attendance and participation in the functions of an average church do not produce or maintain healthy souls. Just look at the condition of some of our churches! The typical pastor supports externals—prescribed activities to care for the soul—putting little emphasis on such internalized pursuits as:

Re-programming the mind
Evaluating our values
Renewing our emotions
Setting our conscience to God's standards
Strengthening our will
Purifying our attitudes
Examining our motives

We need first to be taught about the spiritual indicators needed to check our internal equipment before the care-and-feeding of the soul will seem pertinent.

When people ask me about the condition of my church, I ask, "What measurement do you want? Head (knowledge)? Stomach (numbers)? Or heart (love and faith)?" Not only churches judge "success" by external standards. Individual Christians use similar yardsticks: career recognition, income, house, cars, clothes, college attended, children's performance in school, and frequency of church attendance. Individuals, like churches, can exhibit all the externals of success and yet have damaged souls hanging on the precipice of crisis and calamity. A soul must be properly nourished and exercised if it is to mature and flourish—and I'll have much more to say about the specifics later!

Neglect: Causes of Soul Malnutrition

Why do we neglect so important a matter as spiritual nourishing? "Neglect" implies that we know the facts but fail to apply them, for whatever reason.

In Proverbs 24:30–34, we find a most graphic description of neglect and the accompanying results:

> I passed by the field of the sluggard,
> And by the vineyard of the man lacking sense;
> And behold, it was completely overgrown with
> thistles,
> Its surface was covered with nettles,
> And its stone wall was broken down.
> When I saw, I reflected upon it;
> I looked, and received instruction.
> "A little sleep, a little slumber,
> A little folding of the hands to rest,"
> Then your poverty will come as a robber,
> And your want like an armed man.

There are two reasons we neglect the health of our souls. The first is sheer laziness. We may be lazy for many reasons, but laziness is a vicious cycle: it both causes and results from a diseased soul. Sick souls are like sick bodies. They are so weak-willed, wounded emotionally, and saturated with destructive thoughts that they just lie there without the energy to get moving!

Laziness

Laziness is a manifestation of a weak, damaged, and sick soul. Ironically, when we most need help, we least reach out for it or even know we want it. The nature of temptation includes withdrawal: we want to be alone. Yet we are created to be gregarious and interdependent beings. So our best protection against withdrawal is in building dynamic relationships with people who will help us up when we are down. Such relationships must be developed *before* we need their support for pushing our "on" buttons.

Busyness and Distraction

Or perhaps we are just too involved with "busy-ness" to tend to the needs of our souls, as the following illustrates:

> The most remarkable thing about Holland is its prosperity. Unlike in France, England, or the United States, there are almost no poor people. Wherever you go people look well fed, well dressed, and well housed. This Christmas especially, it seemed that everyone was able to buy what they wanted, eat what they liked, and go where they wished. Countless Dutch people went to Switzerland or Austria to ski; others stayed home eating, drinking, and watching TV, and a few attended well-prepared and carefully orchestrated worship services. The country feels very self-satisfied. There is not much space left, inside or outside, to be with God and God alone.
>
> It is hard to explain why Holland changed from a very pious to a very secular country in one generation. Many reasons can be given. But it seems to me, from just looking around and meeting and speaking to people, that their captivating prosperity is one of the more obvious reasons. People are just very busy—eating, drinking, and going places.
>
> Paul van Vliet, a well-known Dutch comedian, used, as one of the themes in his Christmas TV show, "We are smart but very distracted." Indeed, we know and understand what we most need, but we just don't get around to it, since we are so busy playing with our toys. There is too much to play with! No real time to grow up and do the necessary thing: "Love God and each other."
>
> The Dutch have become a distracted people—very good, kind, and good-natured but caught in too much of everything.
>
> Henri J. M. Nouwen
> *The Road to Daybreak*
> (N.Y.: Bantam, 1988), p. 108

Today, perhaps the most common reason for soul-care neglect among God's people is distraction, our preoccupation with "urgent" superficials. Everybody is so very busy. The pressures of modern-day living relentlessly compete for our time and concentration. It is almost unthinkable that we should add soul maintenance as a regular activity, especially when the results will probably not be immediately apparent.

> We are caught in the tyranny of the present:
> the visible things of the here and now,
> today's opportunities and challenges.

Why worry over the future or even plan wisely the important matters that could change tomorrow for the better?

Someone asked a great leader how he could carry out all his responsibilities and continue to take on new ones. He replied, "I divide these projects into two groups: the imperative and the important. Then I forget the imperative and act on the important."

Sounds backwards doesn't it? But it is not. Seeming imperatives can so distract us that we never get to the really important things. Jesus rebuked Martha for just such an attitude:

> Martha was distracted with all her preparations [for her honored guest]; and she came up to Him, and said, "Lord, do You not care that my sister has left me to do all the serving alone? Then tell her to help me." [Mary sat listening to Jesus' words.] But the Lord answered and said to her, "Martha, Martha, you are worried and bothered about so many things; but only a few things are necessary, really only one, for Mary has chosen the good part, which shall not be taken away from her" (Luke 10:40–41).

Are you so occupied with the physical and temporal that you have no time for the spiritual and eternal?

Some women spend more time on their hair than on
their souls, in direct disregard of Peter's advice: "And let
not your adornment be merely external—braiding the
hair, and wearing gold jewelry, or putting on dresses; but
let it be the hidden person of the heart, with the imperishable quality of a gentle and quiet spirit, which is precious in the sight of God" (1 Peter 3:3). Of course, men,
too, can be so busy with externals, with the abundance
of material things that wealth has afforded them, that
they ignore Jesus' admonition that life does not consist
of the abundance of one's possessions (Luke 12:15).

Burnout

Finally, a less obvious reason for careless neglect of a
soul's nutritional needs is especially relevant for
Christian leaders: clergy and laypersons alike. Sometimes a Christian can become so preoccupied with doing
the work of God among the flocks that his own soul is
allowed to lie dormant or diseased. Certain religious
leaders we have all read about were so busy being "shepherds" that they forgot their own status as creatures in
need of God's care and forgiveness.

Every soul is priceless—of infinite value to the
Creator and to you as an individual. Learning *why* that
is so is the topic of the next chapter.

PART 2

RECOGNIZING A
HEALTHY SOUL

Now I Understand

When I first began to walk on this road
You've brought me to,
I thought the greatest thing would be
To have You use me
To share the wonders of the cross
With the sinner that is lost,
To heal the sick and set the captive free.
But now I understand that when You took
me by the hand,
Your great desire, Lord, was to make me
like Your son,
With a heart to worship and to know Your
presence,
To let Your Spirit form Jesus in me.
All those things I tried to do,
All the words I tried to say,
When all along You just wanted me to love
You;
To enjoy that special time
That would be just Yours and mine—
Every day—learning how You love me.
And now I understand what delights Your
Father's heart.
Not all those things I'd do,
But to come and be with You,
To worship at Your throne,
Spending time with You alone
To let Your spirit form Jesus in me.

Barbara Richmond, 1989

5

The Goal of Soul Care

Charles Atlas epitomized the ultimate of body care a few decades ago. Posing in a swimsuit on the back of every comic book and tabloid, he represented the ideal male body. The picture included an enticing caption promising that anyone could look like him. Although the ad promoted the idea that this potential was hidden in all of us, you could only get such results by buying the advertised product, a set of muscle-building springs.

As a pudgy fourteen-year-old, living in Jamaica, I looked at this picture and then at myself in the mirror. I swallowed the advertiser's bait—hook, line, and sinker. To look like this bronzed he-man became the goal of my body care. I withdrew my meager savings from the bank, entrusting my money to a missionary going on furlough to the States. I could hardly wait for him to bring me a set of the magical springs that would change my small, fat, big-hipped frame into a Charles Atlas body.

The springs arrived, but alas, I never changed into the likeness of Charles Atlas. Two reasons contributed to this failure.

First, the physical genes I inherited would never win me the prize of being a six-footer with narrow hips. To a great degree, hereditary factors had already determined my basic physical makeup.

But the second reason was not predetermined. I presumed that merely owning the springs would re-make me. I ignored the basic fact that using the springs regularly was what developed the muscles and dispelled the fat. You can probably understand why I did not change into what I wanted to be!

We make this same assumption in the religious arena. We often mistakenly think that merely taking truth home changes us. In reality, it is applying that truth, working it into our lives, that makes the difference. Truth should act like a verb—something to do, not a new fact to stick in our heads and let lie there.

Whether the exercise springs could live up to the ad's promise, I would never know, for I barely used them. Because of my neglect, I would never know whether they could have transformed me into a muscle man.

To my generation, Charles Atlas represented the epitome of body care—a goal worth striving for. To the Christian, what is the goal of soul care?

A Test

Before we answer this, let's look at some questions to see how much you know about *yourself,* meaning your *soul.* If you do not know the answer, write out, "I do not know."

1. Why did God create you? What did he intend your primary function to be?

   _____

   _____

2. Why did Christ save you? What was the purpose of your redemption? Complete this statement: "I am saved for

   _____ "

3. What is your ultimate goal in life?

   _____

   _____

4. If you reached your maximum potential as a Christian, what would you be like?

   _____

   _____

5. If you reached your maximum potential as a Christian what would you be doing? What do you think your major functions would be?

   _____

   _____

Purposes and Functions

Just about everything is made with a primary function in mind—that is, its number-one purpose. When we use an object, we are usually aware of its *primary* purpose. To demonstrate this, consider the primary purpose of a pencil, a car, a watch.

Sure, a pencil has an eraser, and its secondary function is to erase. But if it does not write (primary function, or number-one purpose), the secondary function is of no value.

The secondary purposes—beauty, comfort—of a car are of little value if it does not fulfill its primary function: transportation. And a watch that does not tell time, even when its face is surrounded with diamonds, is not really a watch.

All of these objects have secondary purposes that are subordinate to the primary one. If the primary purpose is not fulfilled, any secondary functions are insignificant to the owner.

So it is with man. God had a plan, a definite primary purpose in mind when he made us. Achieving this purpose is the goal of all soul care.

What Is God's Plan?

Beloved, I pray that in all respects you may prosper and be in good health, just as your *soul prospers* (3 John 2, italics mine).

My particular part of the church establishment has heavily promoted the following statement: "We are saved to serve!" This is a very good pry bar or ax handle for getting people to serve. Of course, it is easy to "validate" with prooftexts from the Scriptures. There is enough truth in the statement to make it acceptable, but also enough error to cause all types of spiritual dilemmas and bad behavior.

The present dilemma of our group (one that reflects an almost 50-50 division) comes from each individual's impelling desire to serve God in the way he or she thinks best. Some broadly proclaim the *number-one* priority of Christians to be the Great Commission found in Matthew 28:19–20—evangelism. This seems in plain disagreement with what Jesus said when asked, "What is the greatest commandment?" Jesus said (Matt. 22:36–39), "To love the Lord your God with all your heart, mind, soul, and body, and then to love your neighbor as yourself."

Why *did* God create us in the first place? What does God want us to do? Why did God save us?

When anything is saved, it is redeemed to do what it was created to do, even though (for whatever reason) it stopped operating as originally intended. This summer my watch stopped telling time (what it was made to do). I took it to Charlie, my watch repairman, and he informed me that he could save it (fix it like new). He did, and I know it was fixed, not because he put a tag on it saying it was repaired, but because it is now functioning the way it was intended in the first place.

The apostle John phrased Jesus' "greatest commandment" (Matt. 22:36–39) differently: ". . . we proclaim to you also, that you also may have fellowship with us; and indeed our fellowship is with the Father and with His Son Jesus Christ" (1 John 1:3).

"Fellowship" does not mean merely praying to God at regular intervals or getting together at somebody's house after a church service. All that may be a part of it, but true fellowship is broader than that. It is how *lovers* relate to each other. It is significant that the Greek word for "fellowship" is translated in the King James Version of the Bible to embody such concepts as: communion, contribution, companionship, partnering. It means having common purposes, a binding together in intimacy.

Our main purpose is to love God. Do you? Your answer will probably be yes. But do you really love him with all your heart, soul, mind, and body?

Our Primary Functional Goal: Loving God

Love has lost its meaning in our culture because the sweeping use of the word has diluted and perverted what it implies. But a word that goes along with love is "enjoy." What we enjoy, we love. What we love, we enjoy.

The Westminster Catechism says, "The chief end and duty of man is to love God and enjoy Him forever." If you were to join a Presbyterian church and took its class for new members, you would be expected to repeat that

and mean it, to understand that loving God—our primary purpose—means *enjoying* him.

Do you know many people who enjoy God? Do *you*
think of your faith in terms of enjoying him? Most people's "religion" is a series of activities, not a relationship
that focuses on enjoyment.

Enjoying God does not mean taking pleasure in the
Bible, church services, fellowship with the saints, or
even our ministry. It is enjoying our *fellowship* with
God. If I put the primary purpose of all Christians—the
overall goal of soul care—in a diagram, this is how it
would look:

Cause and Effect

We live in a world of cause and effect. It follows that
the right cause will bring about a desired effect.

Enjoying and loving God are effects. The causes of those effects are seeking and knowing God. Knowing God means far more than knowing *about* him. It signifies knowledge that comes out of a deeply personal relationship with him. The Old Testament and New Testament use the word *know* for the sexual experience between husband and wife, the most intimate human expression of love.

Loving God is the *summum bonum*—the key to everything. Yes, faith is important and so is hope, but the greatest is love.

Love always gives lavishly, joyfully, sacrificially.

Love always works diligently and creatively.

Love always praises sincerely, excitedly, fully.

Love always trusts, believes, counts as true.

Love always sees and hears what no other can hear or see.

Our functional goal is to love and enjoy God and to express that love in the ways he desires. We do that by seeking him. He then reveals himself to us and *we know him.*

Our Character Goal: Being Ourselves

Our functional goal is really dependent on our character goal. If we are not acting out of what we are, then we are play-acting, a pretense that is both difficult and tricky to maintain.

What is the secret? It is to "be"! It is not hard to act like a horse if you are a horse. You just do what comes naturally and instinctively. But it would be difficult (impossible) for a horse to act like a cow. The horse would be under a constant strain. So your character goal is *being* you, a beloved child of the God who made us in his own image and likeness and desires our fellowship.

A few years ago we had a parakeet named "Petie." The little fellow had no one else to play with, so he played with us humans. But one day I got another parakeet and, from that day on, we got little attention from Petie because someone with his own nature arrived. He found someone he could relate to in a better way.

The same is true about God and us. Once born again, we have the same nature as God and the same capacity for fellowship, although that capacity must be developed through the maturing of the inner man. That brings us right back to the subject at hand: the goal of soul care.

My oldest son is thirty-seven. My youngest is nineteen. I have fellowship with them both but on different levels, solely because of maturity and all it brings with it. My oldest son is a husband, a father, a pastor. My other son has none of these responsibilities yet (he probably will). But fellowship increases according to the areas of commonality and character that exist between two people.

Our character goal is to *be* like Jesus—to have the perfect fellowship that Jesus had with his Father God while he was in the body. For Jesus to get to this place of perfect fellowship, he had to grow and mature. The one Scripture that describes Jesus between his birth and earthly ministry is Luke 2:52—"And Jesus kept increasing in wisdom and stature, and in favor with God and men." This is another way of saying he *grew* mentally, physically, spiritually, and socially to become as he was portrayed in the four Gospels—thirty years of growing and three years of ministry.

Paul expressed the need for Christians to grow and mature. For example, to the Romans he said, "For whom He foreknew, He also predestined to become conformed to the image of His Son . . ."(Rom. 8:29).

To the Ephesians Paul said that we are to build up the body of Christ,

> until we all attain to the unity of the faith, and of the knowledge of the Son of God, to a mature man, to the measure of the stature which belongs to the fulness of Christ. As a result, we are no longer to be children, tossed here and there by waves, and carried about by every wind of doctrine, by the trickery of men, by craftiness in deceitful scheming; but speaking the truth in love, we are to grow up in all aspects into Him, who is the head, even Christ, from whom the whole body, being fitted and held together by that which every joint supplies, according to the proper working of each individual part, causes the growth of the body for the building up of itself in love (Eph. 4:13–16).

He addressed the Galatians as "My children, with whom I am again in labor until Christ is formed in you—" (Gal. 4:19).

Peter put it another way: ". . . like the Holy One who called you, be holy yourselves also in all your behavior; because it is written, 'YOU SHALL BE HOLY FOR I AM HOLY'" (1 Peter 1:15–16).

Our character goal is to become like Jesus, to *be* him to the world. We have the potential, all the spiritual genes, to do so. Now we must set out in this direction knowing that it takes time to grow. As long as we are growing, we are succeeding, but the journey (our functional goal) is as important as the destination (our character goal).

Growth is a definable process. This is what soul care is all about. We could diagram it like this:

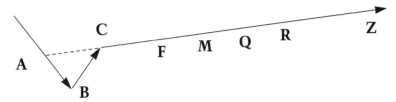

A→Z	represents God's original intention for his beloved children—that we should grow and progress to be like Christ, spiritually united to him.
A→B	is the path we took away from God and his purpose. We sinned and turned from God.
B	is our encounter with Christ. We are born again, baptized into the body of Christ. Though we are given the Holy Spirit, we are not yet at **Z**.
C	starts us back on the path we left. We can now move on to maturity, on to **Z**—the zenith of what we ought to be.
FMQR	represent different phases and stages of maturity. The main trouble is that most never seem to move away from **C**. (And if they do, they often slide back.)

God's Eternal Secret

What did God want in the beginning? He wanted a family of sons and daughters he could love and who would love him in return. His purpose has never changed and it never will. God's plan will be fulfilled with or without us. *He* cannot fail, though each of us may choose whether or not we will fit in. He has already chosen you. Now will you accept his choice of you and let your perfect Father bring you to maturity? That means recognizing that Jesus became what you are, that you might become what he is.

"Success," "happiness," and "a meaningful life" are terms that represent the rewards that come from being and doing what we were created and saved to be—born-again children of God.

Success. True success is doing what you were created to do. A successful pencil is one that writes. A successful automobile is one that gets us where we want to go. A successful Christian is one who loves God and accepts his love and his purposes.

Happiness. The result of doing what we were made to do is happiness. It is a by-product, an inevitable effect. Someone said, "You never find happiness by looking for it. You find it on the road to duty." Want to be happy? Be what you were made to be and do what you were made to do.

A Meaningful Life. Life can have no real meaning unless it is directed toward a purpose, a reason for being. Boredom, laziness, vacillation, fear, doubt—all come out of having no definite purpose in life and continuing that way. When you give your life to doing what it is your nature to do, you will find meaning and fulfillment.

JESUS
IS MY GOAL
AND
MY WAY—
TO BE LIKE HIM AND
THEN LIVE LIKE HIM IS *IT!*

Man is both a spiritual
and an animal being.
One can move a man
either by influencing his animal being
or by influencing his spiritual essence.
In the same way
one can change the time on a clock
either by moving the hands
or by moving the main wheel.
And just as it is better to change the time
by moving the inner mechanism,
so it is better to move a man—
whether oneself or another person—
by influencing his consciousness.

Leo Tolstoy
"Why Do Men Stupefy Themselves?"

6

The Senses of the Soul

In his best-seller, *The Closing of the American Mind,*
Alan Bloom made a statement about today's college students: "As it now stands, students have powerful images
of what a perfect body is and pursue it incessantly. But
deprived of literary guidance, they no longer have an
image of a perfect soul, and hence do not long to have
one."

Bloom is saying that today's value system emphasizes
the physical body, the outer man. We are apparently not
concerned with the inner man. If you are oblivious to
the existence of something—in this case "a perfect
soul"—you certainly will not desire it, much less take
care to attain it.

This is a regrettable commentary about today's secu-
larly oriented youth. Tragically, the typical Christian is
also steeped in the world's value system, even though
the essence of Christianity is its concentration on the
condition of the inner man and the destiny of the soul.

Our basic objective in this section is to review what we already know about the soul (see Part 1) and then pose some related questions:

1. What does a healthy soul look like?
2. What causes a soul to mature?
3. What causes a soul to be sick and unhealthy?
4. What does it take to make a sick soul well?
5. What is soul food, good and bad?

Senses—Physical and Spiritual

What would you do if you had awakened this morning with double vision? Impaired hearing or no hearing at all? Inability to recognize objects by touch or to walk without stumbling? Why, you would (or should) go to see a doctor immediately!

You would be in a panic because of the critical need to have your senses operating normally and your body functioning correctly. Why this panic? Because we relate to the physical world in direct proportion to the operation of our senses and basic bodily functions.

Certain definable indicators are standards for a healthy body. We know about such obvious signs as a sore throat, an earache, or a swollen ankle. But our hidden systems—circulatory, cardiovascular, pulmonary, sensory—only doctors can evaluate adequately. When we have a sore throat, we usually just go to the drugstore and get some throat lozenges. Only when this doesn't help, do we go to a doctor.

Besides telling us whether we are well or sick, our five senses partially determine and measure our general physical condition, how we handle such bodily functions as locomotion, digestion, respiration, and so on. It follows that our performance in the physical world is limited to the degree that our five senses—sight, hearing, touch (and, to a somewhat lesser degree, our taste and smell)—are impaired, immature, or otherwise malfunctioning.

Just as your body's senses enable you to relate to the physical world in an appropriate and meaningful way, so your soul's senses enable you to relate to the spiritual world. To the degree that the senses of your spirit are impaired, to that degree is your soul limited in its ability to communicate with and function in the spirit world.

Furthermore, a healthy soul has the ability to work intimately and function efficiently in *both* realms, physical and spiritual. When we are born again, new life is given to our spirit senses. But the use of these senses needs to be developed, even as the physical senses need to mature in a newborn.

Purity of Heart: The Eyes of the Soul

Stop and think what your life would be without sight! Television is a much more powerful medium than radio because it combines sight as well as sound. The cliché "one picture is worth a thousand words" stresses the high value we place on sight. So it also is in the spiritual world.

Did you know that your soul has eyes? That is why Paul prayed for the Christians "that the eyes of your heart may be enlightened . . ." (Eph. 1:18). What does he mean by this?

Newborns "see," but they do not yet know what they see. They learn to interpret the light waves coming into the brain through the optical nerves. The baby sees Mother but at first does not understand who or what he sees. When he learns to distinguish his mother, he responds in a thrilling way: with a gurgle of delight, a smile, and eventually "Mama."

In much the same way, the eyes of the heart are open to the spirit world, but we must learn how to interpret the light coming in. Spiritually enlightened eyes understand what they see. One of the first things an enlightened soul learns is to identify the Creator God and to respond, "Abba, Father." A person who has never seen with the eyes of the heart might not understand this because, having lived in inner darkness all the time, he does not understand light and accepts darkness as a normal part of life.

Jesus described one of the secrets of his supernatural lifestyle here on earth: "Truly, truly, I say to you, the Son can do nothing of Himself, unless it is something He sees the Father doing; for whatever the Father does, these things the Son also does in like manner" (John 5:19).

Jesus *saw* what was going on in the spirit world through the eyes of his healthy, mature soul. He saw the Father and his activities, as well as demons and angels and their activities. So can we—and so we *must* if we are to live spiritually.

Imagination

From beginning to end, the Bible is full of people who saw visions and dreams while physically awake. What is a vision? It is seeing with the eye of the heart into the spirit world. God sends light and we see. It is as simple as that!

What activates the eyes of the soul? Imagination, the ability of the soul to see what is not present in time or space in a physical or tangible form.

Much writing on "the evils of the imagination" has scared us away from the concept. But imagination is as much a part of the soul as the liver is part of the body. It is a normal, natural function of the soul. *Vain* imaginations are wrong, and they arise because our spiritual vision is clouded.

Worry, for instance, comes from a distorted imagination. Most worries are ghostly images. They are not real, but instead are a false picture projected to the imagination by the evil one. *Real* imaginations (including visions and dreams from God) are not only okay; they are normal and needed, a sign of soul health.

Ignorance and confusion about the spiritual realm tells you something is wrong with the eyes of your soul. This is what Jesus meant when he said, "The lamp of the body is the eye; if therefore your eye is clear, your whole body will be full of light. But if your eye is bad, your whole body will be full of darkness. If therefore the light that is in you is darkness, how great is the darkness!" (Matt. 6:22–23). A defective eye may be one that does not see, that sees double, or that has poor vision in darkness. Darkness brings confusion, which means you do not see clearly and therefore cannot act decisively.

Health Care for the Eyes of the Soul

You can better understand the eyes of the soul if you understand your physical eyes and how they work. A normal functioning eye looks like this diagram:

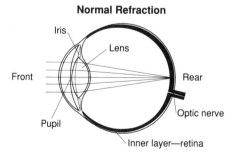

Normal Refraction

Light from the outside enters through an unclouded lens and clearly focuses on the retina. The nerve endings there transmit to the brain, where the light impressions are interpreted.

An eye with a cataract (an impaction of dead cells in the lens) causes cloudy vision. It usually has some sight but cannot clearly distinguish between objects because light is scattered in all directions, as in this diagram:

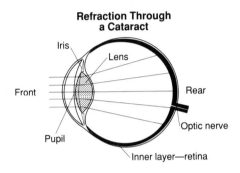

Refraction Through a Cataract

Since the light is not focused on the retina, the impressions that go to the brain are distorted. The result is confusion about what one sees.

Much the same can happen to the eyes of the soul. In speaking to those of Jewish heritage, those who "are confident that you yourself are a guide to the blind, a light to those who are in darkness" (Rom. 2:19), the apostle Paul reminded them that ". . . he is not a Jew who is one outwardly; neither is circumcision that which is outward in the flesh. But he is a Jew who is one inwardly; and circumcision is that which is of the heart, by the Spirit, not by the letter; and his praise is not from men, but from God" (vv. 28–29).

Paul refers to the Holy Spirit's surgical removal from the heart of anything that distorts the ability to view what's happening in the spirit world. When we can see what's happening in the spirit world, we won't be praising men, we'll praise God.

Another way of looking at this is pictured in the diagram Mark Virkler gives in his series on "Communion with God."

Praying With an Idol

"The thing" is held more prominently in your consciousness and vision than is Jesus.

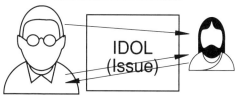

An "idol" is anything or anybody that we hold more prominently in our consciousness than Jesus Christ. Of course, idols cloud the heart's vision. When we try to see God and the spirit world through an idol—through the issue or circumstance that has initiated our prayer—spiritual truth becomes distorted.

The next diagram illustrates what happens when the eyes of a soul is fixed *directly* upon Jesus Christ. When Jesus is number one in our heart, we can view the issue in the full light of his presence, so that nothing interferes with our vision. We see with clarity what *he* wants us to see.

Praying Without an Idol

Jesus is held more prominently in your heart and mind than is "the thing" for which you are praying.

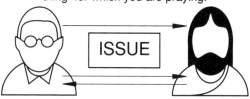

Jesus told us, "Blessed are the pure in heart, for they shall see God" (Matt. 5:8). A pure heart is a circumcised heart, a heart free of idols, a heart that sees God clearly in every situation of life.

Soul health includes the ability to see in the spirit world and to understand, in an ever-increasing way, what we see. To that end, let us pray:

> My God and Father,
>> My Lord and Savior.
> I am grateful for your love and all
>> the expressions of it.
> I desire to have a pure heart to see you
>> and a whole heart to love you perfectly.
> Show me today anything that hinders this.
>> Give me grace not only to see these idols, but also grace to be willing to submit to the Holy Spirit's surgery.
> Holy Spirit, please circumcise my heart
>> that I may love you in a way that brings you pleasure.
> For your glory and pleasure, O God. Amen.

Sincerity of Heart: The Ears of the Soul

When our physical hearing is fully developed, it is incredible what we can hear in our environment. In my book *Hearing God* (Baker, 1988), I tell of a man who can distinguish the sounds of 225 different types of crickets with his naked ear and identify what they are communicating. This man's innate hearing capacity is probably no better than anyone else's, but he has worked very hard to fine-tune it to an extraordinary degree.

On the other hand, we can become unaware of certain sounds simply because we learn to ignore them. People who live next to airports cease to hear the planes overhead, though the blasts of the engines usually startle an occasional visitor to their homes.

Our physical ears receive sounds from a natural, physical world and interpret these sounds according to past experiences. This is how communication in the physical world can take place, since hearing is the basis of language. In a corresponding way, the ears of the soul receive messages from the spiritual world—from God or the evil one. This communication passes on to the soul, where it is interpreted and understood, just as physical sounds are "translated" in the brain.

A newborn child hears but must learn the meaning of the sounds. Similarly, a born-again soul has spiritual ears but has to learn to identify what is being heard.

Our Lord often repeated this phrase: "He who has ears to hear, let him hear" (Matt. 11:15; cf. Matt. 13:9, 43; Mark 4:23; Luke 14:35; Rev. 2:7). Couple this with two other statements he made and you will know how important hearing is to the soul. First he said, "My mother and My brothers are these who hear the word of God and do it" (Luke 8:21).

Later, Mary was sitting at Jesus' feet, *listening* to his every word, and he said to her sister, Martha, that "only a few things are necessary, really only *one,* for Mary has chosen the good part, which shall not be taken away from her" (Luke 10:42).

Jesus indicated two basic truths about "hearing"—the *capacity* to hear, ("he who *has* ears") and the *ability* to hear ("*let* him hear"). The capacity (the hearing apparatus) is given to us. The ability (understanding what is heard) must be developed. He also told us how important that ability is in our lives. All of the New Testament teaching is nonsense if it were not possible for the ears of the soul to hear in the world of the spirit.

In the new birth we are *given* soul ears, but we must *develop* them to understand the language of God. Fortunately, God is a knowing and caring parent who always speaks to his children according to their level of maturity and understanding.

Our general spiritual well-being is in proportion to our ability to hear and thus to relate to the spiritual world. It is normal and natural to hear from God easily and regularly if we have a healthy soul.

Jesus heard and told us he did: "I can do nothing on My own initiative. As I hear, I judge; and My judgment is just, because I do not seek My own will, but the will of Him who sent Me" (John 5:30). Then he acted on the basis of what he heard, reminding us that faith is a necessity of soul life: ". . . he who believes in Me, the works that I do shall he do also . . ." (John 14:12). The apostle Paul wrote on this same theme, the need to learn the language of heaven: "So faith comes from hearing, and hearing by the word of Christ" (Rom. 10:17).

Faith is knowing what is not yet evident in the physical world because we hear about it from God, who is not limited to time and space.

Conscience: The Soul's Sense of Touch

Through our physical sense of touch we relate to the material world in a greater way than we could with eyes and ears alone. Our sense of touch refines our discernment and gives us the ability to distinguish whether something is

safe or dangerous
hot or cold
soft or hard
sharp or dull
present or absent

Even when it is dark and still, we can move around fairly reliably by our sense of touch. The soul also has a sense of touch. It is conscience—the ability of the soul to tell the difference between good and evil.

The Bible talks about many conditions of conscience, some healthy and some diseased. A healthy conscience is described with such words as "blameless" (Acts 24:16), "good" (1 Tim. 1:5), and "clear" (1 Tim. 3:9). In fact, Paul says that a good conscience should be our goal because without it our faith shall suffer "shipwreck" (1 Tim. 1:19).

A bad conscience is described as "weak" and "defiled" (1 Cor. 8:7), "wounded" (1 Cor. 8:12), "seared" (1 Tim. 4:2), and "evil" (Heb. 10:22).

An Overview

In 1 Timothy 1:4, Paul states his goal for writing to Timothy, his "true child in the faith":

A pure heart (one that sees God, cf. Matt. 5:8)
A good conscience (a discerning spiritual sense of touch)
A sincere faith (one that hears God)

What is your rating in these areas? The health of your spiritual senses determines the health of your soul and therefore your ability to succeed in the spirit world.

Jesus' healing of the blind and the deaf indicates to me that he wants us to let him heal our inner blindness and deafness and other immaturities of the soul's capacities. When our spiritual senses are not functioning as they should, we need to come to Jesus and receive his prescription for healing and restoration.

Like children
we are prone to run wildly ahead
of our Father.
He calls out to us
as we run merrily
through the lights of life's carnivals,
"Wait!"
Isaiah pours new energy
into the exhausted hearts
of hasty people
run dry from sprinting
through life's corridors
without pit stops.

"But those who hope in the Lord will
renew their strength.
They will soar on wings
like eagles;
they will run and not be faint"
(Isa. 40:31).

7

Functions of a Healthy Soul

As previously explained, the physical functions of the body—walking, handling, eating, talking—are largely dependent on the proper working of the physical senses. If our senses are impaired, these natural functions are nonoperative or significantly reduced.

It should come as no surprise to you that so it is with the soul! If you wonder why people are often apathetic about spiritual matters, it is because their spiritual senses are immature, malfunctioning, or dead. We cannot act in a "spiritual" manner if we do not see, hear, or otherwise have sensitivity in that dimension.

Healthy Souls Can Walk Well—Holy Lifestyle

The New Testament often uses the word *walk* to describe one's lifestyle—the whole round of activities in an individual's life, whether or not he or she is a

Christian. The term applies to not only "religious" life, but also to conduct and behavior with others.

Did you ever notice that when a Christian sins, it is often called a fall? This is clear indication that Christians who are not walking in spiritually upright ways can stumble along the way, hurting others as well as themselves. So the writer of Hebrews urges us to "strengthen . . . the knees that are feeble, and make straight paths for your feet, so that the limb which is lame may not be put out of joint, but rather be healed [Then we can] pursue peace with all men, and the sanctification without which no one will see the Lord" (Heb. 12:12–14). To do this, we are urged to see "that no one comes short of the grace of God; that no root of bitterness springing up causes trouble, and by it many may be defiled" (v. 15).

A Christian who regularly falls into sin by transgressing the laws of God has weak, nonfunctioning spiritual legs that need to be healed.

Even healthy souls sometimes fall, but not regularly, and they can "run and not get tired . . . walk and not become weary" (Isa. 40:31b)—

1. Walk according to the Spirit (Rom. 8:4)
2. Walk by faith (2 Cor. 5:7)
3. Walk in love (Eph. 5:1)
4. Walk as children of light (Eph. 5:8)
5. Walk worthy of the Lord (Col. 1:10)
6. Walk in wisdom toward outsiders (Col. 4:5)
7. Walk in the light (1 John 1:7)
8. Walk as Jesus did (1 John 2:6)
9. Walk in the truth (2 John 4)

By comparison, the sick, weak, unhealthy soul has unstable legs and

1. Walks according to the flesh (Rom. 8:4)
2. Walks *not* according to love (Rom. 14:15)
3. Walks in craftiness (2 Cor. 4:2)
4. Walks by sight (2 Cor. 5:7)
5. Walks in futility (Eph. 4:17)
6. Walks as an enemy of the cross (Phil. 3:18)
7. Walks in darkness (1 John 1:6)

The promised results that naturally come from walking as we ought include:

We will not carry out lusts of flesh (Gal. 5:16).
We will walk worthily, bearing good fruit (Col. 1:10).
Our walk will please God (1 Thess. 4:1).
Fellowship and cleansing will take place (1 John 1:7).

Paul admonishes us to develop our lifestyle: "Finally then, brethren, we request and exhort you in the Lord Jesus, that, as you received from us instruction as to how you ought to walk and please God (just as you actually do walk), *that you may excel still more*" (1 Thess. 4:1, italics mine). Your soul is healthy if you are walking in the proper Spirit-filled manner in an ever increasing way.

Healthy Souls Are Dexterous

Although "spiritual feet" and "walk" refer to our general lifestyle, "spiritual hands" refers to our soul's dexterity, our actions and attitudes as Christians. We are admonished by the writer of Hebrews to "strengthen the hands that are weak" (Heb. 12:12). A growing, healthy physical body increases in its ability to "handle" things in the physical environment. A healthy soul "handles" things well in the spiritual world.

Handling Relationships

We Christians have not learned to get along with each other. Think of all the arguments within the church that you know about or have even been involved in. By way of example, think of the arguments, fights, and hatred generated by the doctrine of baptism and the indwelling of the Holy Spirit. There are many conflicting ideas about how to experience this "correctly." Isn't it ironic that the Holy Spirit, who desires and works to bring only unity to the church, should indirectly become the subject of so much discord because carnal and immature Christians do not really know him.

The conflicts, disunity, lack of harmony, and moving from one denomination or congregation to another are all demonstrations that:

We have not learned to handle hurt by forgiveness.
We have not learned to love others meaningfully.
We have not learned to handle conflict constructively.
We have not learned how to develop deep friendships.

In short, many of us have spiritual hands that are damaged and thus lack dexterity. Mature Christians easily forgive and accept forgiveness. They know how to love, how to exist with others, how to relate to those who differ. A dexterous soul respects all people and develops deep human relationships.

Handling Responsibility

One of the great needs within the church is a body of mature people who take responsibility and carry it out to fulfillment. For children, carrying out assignments tends to be difficult because they do not want to be committed, tied down. Sick souls in so-called adults cannot carry out responsibilities either. Mature, well souls accept responsibility, carry it out efficiently, and endure over the long haul (faint not).

Handling Scripture

Have you ever wondered how so many people can read the same book, one designed to bring unity, and come up with so many ideas that bring division and disunity? Well, the answer is that they do not know how to handle Scripture. They use it "in craftiness or adulterating the word of God" (2 Cor. 4:2). They use it to argue, beat down, and promote darkness. Peter describes unhealthy souls as "untaught and unstable" people who distort the Scriptures (2 Peter 3:16).

Mature souls understand the need to handle the Word of God wisely. They are ever learning, able to come to a knowledge of the truth and integrate it into their lifestyle. One thing for sure, Spirit-filled people do not fight with each other over Scripture!

Healthy Souls Eat Wisely

Appetite is one sign of a healthy body. Satisfying this appetite through a regular, properly balanced diet of appropriate foods is the path to healthy body maintenance.

Have you ever been to a feed store? There you will find all kinds of plant and animal food—cattle food, hog food, dog food (and puppy, too), horse food, cat food, bird food, grass food, flower food (many kinds).

Every form of life has particular foods best suited for their growth, development, and health. This is true about soul food, too.

The soul is nourished and lives by the words and images it stores. Just as what we eat determines our physical condition, the quality of our spiritual food determines our spiritual condition.

Once food is swallowed, our choice of its effect on the body is over. We can't even decide where it will go. Wouldn't it be wonderful to eat what tastes good and then order the calories to go (or stay) in the body? To tell the ones staying in the body to go to certain parts and become muscles or fat, depending on what we want. This is an impossible dream.

The same is true about the words and impressions we allow into the mind and heart. We can choose what we will let in, but we have no choice about what they will do to us. Improper soul food brings weakness and spiritual disease. Christians will never be healthy, strong, and mature without eating the right soul food and abstaining from the wrong.

Immature people say, "I do not see anything wrong with reading this pornographic book or magazine, watching this violent movie, or listening to this mind-jarring music."

But people desiring a healthy, growing, strong, and stable soul dedicated to the glory of God are particular about their soul food. They eat regularly. They eat right.

> We are what we eat,
> mentally and spiritually
> as well as physically.

This is what Jesus meant when he said, "It is written, 'MAN SHALL NOT LIVE ON BREAD ALONE, BUT ON EVERY WORD THAT PROCEEDS OUT OF THE MOUTH OF GOD'" (Matt. 4:4).

Healthy Souls Need Rest

Healthy bodies need rest for renewal, and so do healthy souls. Ironically, though lack of sleep over a long period hurts us physically, sick people often have a hard time sleeping even when they are in bed. So, too, do weak souls struggle to be at rest.

Healthy souls know how to rest, are able to rest, and take time to rest. Healthy souls know that the will, mind, and emotions have limited amounts of energy and have to be regularly refreshed through spiritual rest and renewal.

Because healthy souls know the dangers of coming short of the grace of God, they recognize that the commandment to rest on the Sabbath was intended so that man would stop and take care of his soul.

Spiritual rest is being able to cast all your cares on the Lord. It is the ability to come boldly before the throne of grace to find mercy and peace in time of need. It is the ability to wait on the Lord—to be trusting, not anxious.

Healthy souls know how to balance rest and work, how to set aside time alone with God, even if it temporarily interrupts their work for God. Healthy souls know when and how to get into the closet and shut the door, and be with the Father in secret. Healthy souls know that if their outgo exceeds their income, their upkeep becomes their downfall. Rest is a function of a healthy, maturing soul.

Conclusion

We've briefly glanced at what a healthy soul looks like, how it receives through its senses, and how it functions. Often we consider people who are like this to be "super-saints." This is not so; they are just saints. But the degree and quantity of sick, weak, immature saints make the few normal saints appear to be super-saints. If we give our soul proper care, all of us can be.

PART 3

ACHIEVING A
PROSPEROUS SOUL

What would happen if,
in some great church convention,
all business were laid aside
and the congregation
were to go to desperate prayer?
If it be objected,
"But we have gathered
to attend to church business,"
we would reply,
"What bigger business
do we have right now
than to turn to God
in holy desperation?" . . .

It would be a mockery and a farce
to assemble a congregation
of disinterested and unconcerned
church members for prayer
just because somebody . . . issued
a proclamation.
Better a handful of souls
who know what time it is. . . .
Start with yourself, get right with God,
and then seek others
of like mind and heart. . . .

What time is it?
It is time for holy desperation
because it is too late for anything else.

Vance Havner
In Times Like These

8

Responsibility for Soul Care

The Holy Spirit places in the heart of all true Christians a strong desire to be holy, to be all God wants us to be, to do all we perceive God wants us to do. When we don't experience the changes we know are necessary, we become frustrated. We futilely try different methods, formulas, and prescriptions, increasing our sense of frustration. The answers found effective for others fail to make any difference in our lives or give any real satisfaction.

This repeated sense of falling short is followed by a weary hopelessness. We might never verbalize, "I give up," but that is our inner conclusion. We conclude that the standards presented as realities in the Scriptures and the lives of a few other Christians are not possible for *us* in this life.

At this point, we take various avenues. Some plod on, but resign themselves to the belief that real inner change is not possible. This is especially true of full-time church workers, those paid to do the job.

Others give up and drop out, believing there is no use in going on if there is no chance of making progress in the right direction. Those with more determination push on, but many eventually burn out.

In *The Closing of the American Mind*, Alan Bloom writes, "America has no-fault automobile accidents, no-fault divorces, and it is moving with the aid of modern philosophy toward no-fault choices." One of the implications he makes is "If I am not responsible for myself, or my decision, I can place the blame elsewhere." Is this valid? Can I blame my inner condition on my parents, culture, wife, job, or even on God?

Who is responsible to care for my soul? Me alone? Is it God's responsibility? Is it the church's job? Accountability must be clearly defined, because anything that is everybody's responsibility is, in essence, nobody's. Then we either pass the buck to someone else or assume responsibilities we should not.

God + Church + You

In the management of a household, the responsibilities for specific chores need to be assigned. If they are not, each member of the household will assume that another person should do it. The result? Little is accomplished. A successful household runs smoothly because there are defined and *divided* responsibilities. Each member understands and carries out his or her part.

So it is with soul care. The responsibility for soul care is threefold:

1. God's responsibility
2. the church's responsibility
3. your own responsibility

If your soul is going to be cared for adequately, God, the church, and you need to carry out your respective responsibilities. To do *your* part, you must know what it is. Otherwise, you will not do it or (even worse) you will try to carry out responsibilities for which you are not equipped or have no authority.

We must first look at soul-care responsibility from these three points of view, remembering that all three agents work *together.*

God's Responsibility: Provision

The primary responsibility for soul care rests with God.

As Father, he is responsible for molding his children's development.

As Lord, he is responsible for instilling in his people obedience.

As Shepherd, he is responsible for ensuring his sheep's safety.

As Guide, he is responsible for setting his followers' pathmarks.

As Teacher, he is responsible for his students' instruction.

As Doctor, he is responsible for prescribing for his patients' spiritual health.

God has the major part in soul care, not only because of his one-on-one relationship to each of us, but also because only he can do the fundamental inner things that need to be done to care for our souls.

God alone can make us godly, mainly because God alone can give us his agape love—and we only love him and others because he first loved us.

Scripture teaches that God has taken upon himself certain responsibilities. Paul says, "For I am confident of this very thing, that He who began a good work in you will perfect it until the day of Christ Jesus" (Phil. 1:6).

Jude echoes with: "Now to Him who is able to keep you from stumbling, and to make you stand in the presence of His glory blameless with great joy" (Jude 24).

Then the writer of Hebrews tells us how God is going to fulfill his responsibility for our soul care:

> I will put my laws into their minds, and I will write them upon their hearts. And I will be their God, and they shall be my people. And they shall not teach everyone his fellow citizen, and everyone his brother, saying, "Know the Lord," for all shall know me, from the least to the greatest of them (Heb. 8:10b–12a).

Most New Testament verbs about "change" are in the passive voice. This means we do not change ourselves strictly by our own initiative; we are changed, which indicates that God will do his part. God's faithfulness is an indelible part of his character. He can be fully counted on to do all he has promised to do—perfectly and on time.

I'm sure you are asking, "If this is true, how come I am not any further along than I am?" The answer is that *you*, too, have a responsibility in the care of your soul. You can either release God to do his part or you can prevent God from doing so. He will not do what he wants to do (and can do) without your cooperation.

If God has the major responsibility for your soul care, you must give him time to do it. Time spent with God is measured by its quality, not by the clock. And it is quite possible to spend "quality time" in Bible study and never get close to God. The Pharisees did this, but Jesus said: "You search the Scriptures, because you think that in them you have eternal life; and it is these that bear witness of Me; and you are unwilling to come to Me, that you may have life" (John 5:39–40).

Jesus was referring to quality time with God when he said, ". . . when you pray, enter into your inner room, and when you have shut your door, pray to your Father who is in secret, and your Father . . . will repay you" (Matt. 6:6).

The Church's Responsibility

From sermons and articles in church publications, members often are reminded of their responsibility to their particular church. While this is a vital factor if a church is to be healthy, the responsibility must be reciprocal if the member is to be healthy. Otherwise, the church is not really a church.

Why should a person join a church? What advantage is there in belonging to a church? What are the benefits for a member?

One of the main tasks of the church is offering watchcare to those who become a part of her. The church says to its members, "Come, we will watch over your soul. We will give the care and advice that is necessary to help you to be whole before God and in your relationships with fellow human beings."

Churches need to move from only being concerned about the strong, the rich, and those who are able to help build successful programs. A true church is one who aims to:

Lovingly go after people when they have been absent.

Have a system in place that clearly identifies when a person does not attend.

Have a budget, not only for salaries, buildings, and literature, but also for helping those members who need temporary (or long-term) financial assistance.

Have a special plan for helping widows, single mothers, and orphans.

Make sure all members are treated the same way, regardless of their financial position.

Christians cannot grow to maturity without a church that aggressively provides the necessary ingredients for effective watch-care.

Nevertheless, no church can do its job of winning and preserving healthy souls without the full cooperation of its membership. For us, that means working for our mutual purpose of "being Christ" for the world by spending quality time toward that end. This kind of time requirement is not fulfilled because we occupy a pew at worship services or attend each and every Sunday school pageant or church supper.

Quality time at church means spending meaningful hours with our brothers and sisters in Christ. It is a time of participation—of give and take—a time of interaction and intimacy.

Our Responsibility: Appropriate Responses

We have a part in the care of our soul—a definite part, a definable part, an achievable part, a vital part.

God and his church will do their part, but we must react suitably. The simple but amazing truth is that genuine Christianity is a response to God in an appropriate, timely way.

Basically we are not initiators but responders, and our lives are determined by the way we react to any part of our environment. Evil is a part of that environment. So is God. *I* determine what kind of person I am by my response to both parts of my environment. I can choose to respond negatively to God: I can ignore him or reject him. Or I can receive him. All of my responses will affect me in varying ways.

A speaker at our church once remarked that great saints are great receivers. Something inside of me rose up and shouted, "No!" because I had been raised in a religious culture that taught that great saints were great *achievers*. My spiritual failures at that time were mostly due to that false concept. Since that time, I have found that the speaker was right, and my life's verse has become "Those who *receive* the abundance of grace and of the gift of righteousness will reign in life through the One, Jesus Christ" (Rom. 5:17b, italics mine).

Receiving is the appropriate response to God, the great Giver.

To be a genuine maturing Christian does not take *my* initiative. I need do nothing but respond in acceptance of God's initiative:

Obedience is response to God's will.
Faith is response to God's promises.
Thanksgiving is response to God's goodness.
Praise is response to God's revealed character.
Sharing is response to God's benevolent love.
Joy is response to God's gift of hope.

All I am asked to do is to respond to God properly. The totality of my response is called worship.

Choosing to Will His Will

An individual's capacity to choose is his or her most God-like characteristic. When God designed us, he gave us the ability and the right to make decisions. He will not force us to do anything.

When Adam and Eve were in the Garden, they had a choice. Everything was theirs to use except the tree of the knowledge of good and evil. Regarding this tree, God had said, "No!" Then he stated the result of disobedience: "You shall surely die if you eat." But because he wanted them to have a choice, God did not build a fence around the tree.

Why did God present an opportunity for evil? The answer is simple. *Love always involves a choice.* Although God loves us and wants our love in return, he will not force love, because then it would not be love. Without an opportunity to choose, the capacity to choose is meaningless. We can decide to demonstrate a positive response to his love by loving, trusting, and obeying him.

When individuals choose to become Christians, they accept Jesus as Lord. But they must still decide whether to obey him in each situation and thus demonstrate the totality of their love. That is why Fénelon said, "Pure religion resides in the will alone."

So many of us live mainly in our feelings rather than in our will. Our feelings come from our reasonings or our emotions, or some mixture of both. Both our reasonings and our emotions are a result of our experiences, encounters, and learning. But to live in the will means that I choose God's way, rather than relying on what I think or want.

Usually our problem is not ignorance of God's will, but refusing to do God's will. God never asks us to do something we cannot do, so the choice is ours—we must decide.

Steps to a Liberated Will

(The following suggestions for freeing the will are from DeVern Fromke's book *Unto Full Stature.*)

Step 1: I must accept the responsibility for what I am and what I have done.

An ancient and familiar temptation is trying to blame our condition on someone else or on a set of circumstances, which is what Adam and Eve did. But Henry Drummond refutes such claims: "Let no one deny that surroundings, people, and places can and do influence us. But only that part of the environment to which we respond influences us. We do the responding. The choice is always ours" (Natural Law in the Spiritual World).

DeVern Fromke has put it this way: I am responsible for how I respond. I have that choice and I make that choice. Until I accept responsibility, I will place the blame elsewhere, and I will never mature.

Step 2: I must discover the place and effectiveness of the will as God designed and intended it to function.

God gave us the right to choose, and he will never take that right from us. It is not what my mind thinks, or what my emotions feel, that changes me. It is what my will chooses.

Some people know they need to lose weight for good health and want to lose weight, but they never do. It is not the knowing or desiring that will cause them to shed pounds. It is choosing to follow a defined diet plan. Until that choice is made, they will lose no weight.

A. W. Tozer explains this from the spiritual point of view: "At what point then, does a theological fact become for the one who holds it a life giving truth? At the point where obedience begins. When faith gains the consent of the will to make an irrevocable commitment to Christ as Lord, truth begins its saving illuminating work, not one moment before."

Until I choose to do what God has ordered for my spiritual well-being, I will not be a healthy, growing soul. Sermons, desires, and understanding of God's truths do not change me. It is my choice to act on those truths that makes the difference.

Step 3: I must understand the importance of the full liberation of the will as it cooperates with the Holy Spirit.

A growing, maturing, soul is not one with a strong enough will to always make the right choices. But it is a soul with a will that is ready to act on the Holy Spirit's instructions. God asks me to submit my will to his will. Then he is released to do what I cannot do in my own strength.

To cure his leprosy, Naaman was instructed by the prophet Elisha to dip seven times in the Jordan River—something he could do if he *chose* to do it, although pride and reason almost kept him from it. When he did as the Lord commanded, he was cleansed of leprosy. It was not human willpower that healed him. It was God's power. Naaman released God by choosing to do what God asked him to do through Elisha. (See 2 Kings 5:1–15.)

Here is how this might work today. A friend is upset with me and is avoiding me. I know he is offended, and I desire to restore the relationship. As I pray about it, God tells me to write a note expressing my admiration of my friend and how I miss our fellowship. This is something I can do. I cannot control what my friend is thinking, but I can write a note. It is up to God to change my friend's mind—to do what only God can do. My part is always to will to do his will.

Step 4: I must learn to live in the will.

I must live in the will and not in my emotions or reasonings. Over and over again I must choose to will the way God has given me: to do as he would do, according to what he has said. I must step away from the temptation to resort to my emotions or my limited knowledge of a situation.

Soul Care Takes Time

"Regularity is a law of spirituality," writes DeVern Fromke. In fact, regularity is a law for all growing, healthy life forms. Eating regularly, exercising regularly, and sleeping regularly are necessary for maximum physical health. A child cannot make himself grow even one inch. But if he accepts his parents' will that he eat and exercise properly, he will reach his growth potential.

We cannot maintain spiritual health by occasional and irregular exercises for the soul. That takes *time*, of course, that four-letter word tied to disciplines of any type. It is a word that we rarely want to hear, but it is not optional.

Yes, soul care takes time—quality time. I can hear you screaming, "I don't have enough time as it is, and you are asking for more?" Sorry, but that is the way it is.

It takes time to do anything, especially anything worthwhile—to take care of your car, to take care of your home, to take care of your body. If you are not prepared to take time, soul care will never happen. Think of it like this: Once you give your life to Christ, you are really giving your time to him. Life *is* time, but you can choose whether it will be productive time.

Making a reasonable assumption that God granted you life for sixty-seven years, how would you spend it? An average person spends it like this:

Three years getting an education
Eight years recreating and relaxing
Six years eating
Five years riding in a car
Four years talking
Fourteen years working
Three years reading
Twenty-four years sleeping

How much time do you give God? If you went to church weekly and prayed for five minutes every morning and evening, you would be giving only five months to God—five months out of sixty-seven years!

"Remember the sabbath day, to keep it holy. Six days you shall labor and do all your work, but the seventh day is a sabbath of the LORD your God . . ." (Exod. 20:8–10). It is significant that in a document as important as the Ten Commandments, God referred to a division of time. This basic guideline is that six days be spent for the physical and material elements of life and one day be devoted to the spiritual realm.

Because God knows he placed us in a physical world with a physical body needing care, he allotted a considerable amount of time for this. But he knew how easy it would be for us to be taken up with these physical demands, so he commanded us to set aside time for the spiritual self: one-seventh, in fact.

Let's think of this, not as a rule, but as a principle God gives for your total welfare, to help you take care of *all* of you. Following this principle, you would give God and spiritual matters the equivalent of one day a week. The average person sleeps eight hours a day. This leaves sixteen hours a week devoted to God and spiritual matters, sixteen hours a week for the well-being of your inner man—your soul.

The exercises I will suggest for soul care could easily be done in this time. Here is a suggested division:

Exercise One—seven hours a week (one hour a day) for God alone

Exercise Two—five hours a week for church (three for the corporate church service, two for the small group)

Exercise Three—three to four hours a week for ministry to others.

Scripture, observation, and experience convince me that if we all practiced this time division, our soul health would increase significantly.

Quality Time Produces Intimacy

It is quite possible for two people to spend large amounts of time together over the course of years and never really know each other—never have achieved intimacy—because what they spent was not *quality* time.

One summer evening during our church retreat, an elderly woman came to me for counseling and prayer. She told me she had been married for fifty-four years to a man she considered a kind husband and good provider, yet she felt that she did not really know him. Although they had spent a lot of good times together, raising their children, fishing, gardening, and enjoying other mutual hobbies, she said, "He never shares with me what is really going on inside of him. There's never been a time when we both sat down and shared from the depths of our souls." She expressed an emptiness, a void in their relationship. They had not spent enough quality time together to experience a true intimacy.

Married couples often come to me for help in salvaging what remains of their shattered relationship. We usually discover that if any real communication ever existed, it died years before. First I begin pushing the partners to be open and honest with each other (and with me). Then I help them understand how to be open and honest with God. Once they begin, a floodgate opens and a wonderful discovery of themselves and each other takes place. This is intimacy in process. It represents each soul moving toward growth, health, and maturity.

Intimacy is a process, not an event measured by the clock. We must be honest, open, and vulnerable with each other, but first this must happen with God. We must not only give God so many minutes, we must open our inner, hidden being to him.

Quality Time Focuses on the Precious Present

Bill Colle, our minister of worship tells our congregation to "be present where you are." During the worship service, he wants them to put aside thoughts of the Sunday pot roast, the hurry of getting a family dressed for church, the out-of-balance checkbook, or whatever else has their attention. Laying aside other concerns and interest and giving your undivided attention to what you are doing—giving your emotions, mind, will, and body to the project at hand—is also a facet of quality time.

A man does not give quality time to his wife while reading the newspaper. Neither does she give quality time to her children while watching television or talking to someone on the telephone.

Similarly, you cannot give quality time to God while dodging cars on a freeway. Yes, you can pray (and probably ought to at this time), but this is not quality prayer. It lacks the opportunity for intimacy because part of your attention is elsewhere.

You cannot give quality time unless you are prepared to give all of yourself, not just a part.

All of you—body, soul, and spirit.
All of you—mind, emotions, and will.
All of you—being fully present where you are.

Making and Taking Time

You are going to have to *make* time and *take* time by strength of will if you want quality time for your soul care. This, too, involves choice. To "make time," you plan it into your schedule, giving certain matters top priority. This really means taking time, because you cannot make more time than there is. There are only twenty-four hours a day to spend. To "take time" means to give up something else you have been doing. Time cannot be manufactured, borrowed, or saved. It is only spent.

Habits and Time

Most of us have habits, established ways of spending our time. Whether good or bad, these habits become binding behavior patterns. To change a habit is not easy. It takes willpower, effort, and time (perhaps six weeks of concentration) to replace an old habit with a new one. The hardest part of starting anything new and different is giving up the old.

To take time for the kingdom of God within us is to seize it by force. This is part of what Jesus meant when he said, "And from the days of John the Baptist until now the kingdom of heaven suffers violence, and violent men take it by force" (Matt. 11:12).

Soul care *means* quality time, *demands* quality time, *is worthy of* quality time, and *cannot take place without* quality time.

> The main thing is
> to keep THE MAIN THING
> the main thing!

Time Facts

There is a dichotomy in many Christian minds. Did you ever say by word or deed, "I can give my life to Christ, but not my time"? This is disastrous. If your life is truly God's, then your time is totally his.

This presents a problem, because most of us complain

that we do not have enough time to do all we ought to do (another deception of the devil). Instead, consider some facts about time:

1. There *is* enough time to do all you ought to do. God knows there are only 24 hours in each day and 168 in every week. He puts them there, so he would be unreasonable to expect more of you than you have time to do. And God is never unreasonable!

2. There is *not* enough time to do all you want to do or other people expect you to do. You have to make a choice.

3. Everything worthwhile takes time. Relationships take time to build and keep healthy. Christianity involves our relationships with God and others.

4. If you choose to do what you ought to do, you will not have time to do what you should not do. The best way to keep from evil is to do good.

5. You have the same amount of time as anybody else, including the President of the United States.

6. The way you spend "free time" (the time you have a choice about) is a good indication of your value system, what you think is important.

You have been spending every bit of your time now—168 hours every week of your life—exchanging it for something every time you use it. By how you regularly spend it, you have established a lifestyle.

Growing as a person is always a result of what you do with your time. Your soul's growth will be implemented by a change in your lifestyle, a change in how you use each precious moment.

A commercial I recently saw flashing on the TV screen shows men and women trying to buy a bit of time. It catches the plight of most of us in our hurry-scurry world. "I don't want a 40-hour week," said Nicholas Murray Butler, former president of Columbia University. "I want a 40-hour day."

I never cease to marvel at how some people, working with the same number of hours we all have, seem to get so much more done. How do they do it? For one thing, they don't squander the bits and pieces of time that punctuate the days. Rather than wasting energy getting irritated while waiting for a call-back from a repair person, they capture those moments creatively. They keep tools handy—a pen, a book, a pair of scissors, a needle, whatever.

Clement C. Moore was a teacher of classical languages. In the course of his career, he published a Hebrew dictionary and was a major benefactor of the General Theological Seminary in New York City. But it is not for the seminary or his dictionary that he is remembered. It is for a set of verses dashed off in 1822 in an hour of Yuletide inspiration—verses he stuffed away as if of no importance. The magic lines begin: "'Twas the night before Christmas, when all through the house. . . ." They never brought Moore a penny, but they did bring him immortality.

Such constructive use of time is available to us all. A Seattle businessman carries a briefcase in which he has paper and envelopes for writing personal letters. In odd moments he keeps countless friendships alive. A woman I know memorized the Sermon on the Mount while commuting to work. A bedspread in our home was quilted by my mother-in-law who, though extremely busy, somehow found minutes to prepare a beautiful gift full of memories for her family.

Remember, most time is wasted in minutes, not hours. The average person diddles away enough minutes in ten years to have earned a college degree.

Thinking of this reminds me of a verse from my childhood by Julia Fletcher Carney:

> Little drops of water,
> Little grains of sand,

Make the mighty ocean
And the pleasant land.

Do you recall the next four lines?

So the little minutes,
Humble though they be,
Make the mighty ages
Of eternity.

Adapted from *Reader's Digest,*
"How to Find Time" by Dale Turner
Condensed from *Seattle Times* (October 1, 1988)

Conclusion

No time = No soul care
Quality time = Quality soul care

Are you prepared to pay the price?

*Therefore let us inculcate
in ourselves and in our children
the means of achieving mental
and spiritual health.
By this I mean
let us teach ourselves and our children
the necessity for suffering
and the value thereof,
the need to face problems directly
and to experience the pain involved.
I have stated that discipline
is the basic set of tools required
to solve life's problems.*

*When we teach ourselves
and our children discipline,
we are teaching them and ourselves
how to suffer
and also how to grow.*

M. Scott Peck
The Road Less Traveled

9

The Discipline Directive
A Choice

Fred jogs down my street three or four mornings a week. Sweat pours, covering his body. Agony is written on his face. Why does he subject himself to such torture?

Simple. He is under a self-imposed discipline, mindful that health experts highly recommend exercise to care for the cardiovascular system.

One dictionary states: *"Discipline:* training that corrects, molds, or perfects the body, the mental faculties, or moral character."* Disciplines are planned functions that develop inborn qualities to full potential.

The Nature of Discipline

It bears repeating that we live in a world of cause and effect. That is, if you want certain *effects*, or results, the way to get them is to discover and activate the *causes*, or conditions, that automatically bring those effects.

If you want to produce oranges (effects), you must know how oranges grow (causes) and work with that information. In due time you will have a crop of oranges. You cannot make even one orange, but you can cooperate with the known facts about the life of an orange to encourage your orange tree to bear fruit.

Disciplines of the Christian life are the ways we cooperate with God to mature his life in us so that our soul reaches its fullest potential. By the new birth, we have gained the potential to be like Jesus Christ, to reap the fruits of the Holy Spirit, pleasing God and being in many ways attractive to other people in our world.

Richard Foster, author of the classic, *Celebration of Discipline,* explains that "God has given us the disciplines of the spiritual life as a means of receiving his grace. The disciplines allow us to place ourselves before God so he can transform us." The apostle Paul also wrote about Christian discipline:

> In pointing out these things to the brethren, you will be a good servant of Christ Jesus, constantly nourished on the words of the faith and of the sound doctrine which you have been following. But have nothing to do with worldly fables fit only for old women. On the other hand, discipline yourself for the purpose of godliness; for bodily discipline is only of little profit, but godliness is profitable for all things, since it holds promise for the present life and also for the life to come. It is a trustworthy statement deserving full acceptance (1 Tim. 4:6–9).

Paul's advice to Timothy includes both cause and effect:

Condition (cause): Discipline yourself for the purpose of godliness (soul care).

Results (effects): Godliness is to our advantage—profitable not just for the sweet bye and bye (eternity) for the nasty now and now (life in the flesh).

Paul also presented this concept to the Corinthians: "Do you not know that those who run a race all run, but only one receives the prize? Run in such a way that you may win. And everyone who competes in the games exercises self-control in all things. They then do it to receive a perishable wreath, but we an imperishable" (1 Cor. 9:24–27).

Those who want to win must exercise self-control (discipline) in all areas. Olympic runners exercise self-control in all areas of life, not just in running practice. They eat the right food, do special exercises, get adequate rest, and keep the right mental attitude.

The Christian concerned about having a "winning" soul—one conformed to the image of Christ—disciplines himself in everything. No one can live as a Christian in one area of life but in other areas do un-Christlike things that counteract the flow of grace. This would be like a person trying to be healthy by eating nutritious food at regular mealtimes and pigging out on junk food at odd hours.

Many serious Christians make an effort to practice the right disciplines needed to develop their Christian life but are at the same time destroying it by bad habits, such as what they read or watch on TV.

The Proper Use of Discipline

In beginning *Celebration of Discipline*, Richard Foster solemnly warns about the real possibility that disciplines can become "laws" and the results when this happens. Disciplines become laws when:

We try to force them on others as necessary for a relationship with God.

We use them to manipulate and control people.

We use them to judge others, deciding that their Christianity is good or bad by their adherence to certain behavior.

They bring division or pride.

Proper disciplines place us into a dynamic relationship with Jesus Christ and that is where and how we are changed.

The three Christian disciplines suggested in chapters 10–12 are exercises for the soul, designed to:

1. Help you have personal intimacy with Jesus Christ.

2. Be practiced in varying degrees of time and intensity according to your spiritual maturity. (For the physical body, walking is considered a good exercise. But different people should walk different distances and at different speeds. This is determined by age, present physical condition, and desired results.)

3. Be practiced according to your personal style. (Beginners need basic instructions, their own style develops over time.)

Charting a Soul's Growth

Do you build a soul or grow one? What is your opinion? There *is* a difference, and failure to understand this difference is the basic cause for the unhealthy spiritual condition of many Christians.

When something is "built," all features of the product are determined by the builder, who designs and develops the finished product according to his own plans and desires. Houses are built. From start to finish they are the product of builder-architects. They determine a structure's size, shape, and type of materials used, and then control the time schedule. Only inorganic (dead) things (such as houses, furniture, or cars) are *built.*

Growing is a different matter. When you grow any-thing, you cooperate with a pre-existing life. This life form has a built-in design that may be developed and matured, but not fundamentally changed.

Long ago the Chinese wrapped the feet of their young female children. The bindings did not change the foot into a finger (something else entirely), but only made it deformed and shorter. The bones in the foot continued growing to a predetermined length in spite of the wrap-pings. The finished product was *predetermined* to be a foot. The abnormal environment, the wrappings, pro-duced an abnormal foot, but it was still a foot.

An acorn contains the invisible life forces of an oak. When this life is released and nature cooperates by pro-viding the proper environment, in time the acorn becomes an oak tree.

All organic living things must be *grown*. They cannot be built. It follows, then, that souls are grown, not built. A born-again Christian has the invisible life of God within him. This life has all the spiritual genes neces-sary for forming that person into the character likeness of Jesus. Soul care means providing the optimum condi-tions for soul growth—the environment where this life can flourish.

Heredity vs. Environment

Why are there no coconut trees in Michigan? No polar bears in Texas? No sharks in freshwater lakes? The simple answer to these questions contains the basic principle that every life form is designed for an appropri-ate environment, one in which the life form will grow, mature, and maintain health. The application of this environmental principle to soul care is essential. All our efforts are in vain if we ignore this truth, because here we are dealing with the highest of life forms—life given to us by our Creator, God the Father. We are born of God. He determines our heredity.

Jesus illustrates this when he asks, "Which of you by worrying can add one cubit to his stature?" (Matt. 6:27, NKJV). A person's potential height is determined at the moment of conception. It is a part of his or her inheritance.

Human *heredity* is the transmission of a genetic potential by parents to their offspring. These qualities are instantaneously determined at the moment of conception. We cannot change these factors (though some scientists are trying to). The color of our eyes, our hair type, our height, shape of our bodies, and other physical characteristics are inherited, as are some mental aptitudes.

Human *environment* consists of the physical surroundings and external cultural conditions that influence human life and development. In more general terms, it represents all forces surrounding and acting on any organism for its survival (reaching its potential) or for its deterioration (short-circuiting its potential).

God's plan matches heredity with environment so that each species may thrive. Environmentalists recognize that without the right environment a particular species will not survive. So they act to protect the species by providing the optimum environment.

Agriculture is the science of learning how to cooperate with different forms of plant life so that each reaches maximum growth and develops to its fullest potential. When my oldest son, Richard, was born, I was employed plowing peanuts on a central Florida farm. Seventeen years later, when my son John was born, I visited this farm. They were producing far more peanuts with less labor on the same acreage. Why? Because they had learned how to cooperate with peanut life in a better way. Agriculture does not create life; it cooperates with predetermined life forces.

Chicken farmers have learned how to cooperate with chicken life. They know what it takes to grow a chicken from a tiny hatchling to a market-ready pullet in the cheapest, fastest way. They know how much food and what kind, optimum temperatures and light, and how long the process takes. Scientifically, they know how to cooperate with chicken life to maximize its potential.

The questions at the beginning of this chapter about coconut trees, polar bears, and sharks have one basic answer. These species are not found in those particular places because the environment there is not suited for their survival and prosperity. Each life form has particular environmental needs. The same is true for the soul. We cannot control our spiritual genes, but we can control the soul's environment.

A Lesson from My Avocado Tree

Outside our bedroom is a twenty-foot avocado tree with a couple hundred large avocados on it. It is a continual reminder to me of the importance of environment to any life form.

Years ago this tree started as a seed in a glass of water in our kitchen window. The seed began to grow, roots down, a shoot up. Soon it became too big for the glass, so we planted it outside the bedroom window. That was twelve years ago.

The tree has had serious setbacks. Three unusually cold Florida winters have frozen it so severely that we wondered whether it would survive, since we knew that avocado trees cannot take continued exposure to freezing weather.

But this year is the first year of fruit. And what fruit!

Three very mild winters in succession have given the tree a chance to develop. Here are the lessons I see daily:

1. Avocados (the fruit) come from avocado life forces.
2. Avocado life (in the seed) plus the right environment and time will eventually produce avocados.
3. The wrong environment for avocado life can kill it or give it a severe setback that takes much time to overcome.

Nobody has avocado groves in our Florida town, Titusville, because the environment is too unpredictable. If I were serious about growing avocado trees, I should do it in a more conducive environment, Miami, for instance. As it is, I am not serious about avocados in general. If they grow, fine. If they do not, also fine.

Everything true about the avocado tree is true about our soul, our spirit life. Why take a chance on something that is vitally important? Give your soul's life a chance!

Environment and the Soul

When the environment is hostile to a life form, we must give it extra-special care: special provision and special protection.

> We live in a world environment
> that has always been hostile
> to the life of God.
> The world once threatened
> that life in Jesus,
> as it now threatens God's life in us.

A "friendly" environment is absolutely necessary to sustain life. No organism is self-sufficient. Just as every living thing must have a proper environment, so it is with the redeemed soul. The life of God in us must have positive surrounding conditions if it is to flourish. The soul deteriorates and becomes perverted in a negative environment.

One of environment's greatest contributions to an organism is providing the appropriate food. Every living thing needs the right kind of food to grow, mature, and stay healthy. The soul is no exception.

Since environment not only maintains life, but can modify it, a life form may become abnormal. In nature, the environment can so act on an organism that it becomes a caricature of what it was created to be.

One tragic example of the effects of a hostile environment was seen in the early 1960s. The tranquilizer thalidomide, when taken during pregnancy, affected the normal growth pattern of unborn babies, resulting in abnormally shortened limbs.

Just as our body responds to environmental influences, our soul responds to our spiritual environment, good or bad. The perverted type of "Christianity" we see so often today is mainly a result of living in an adverse environment. The soul will not mature in hostile surroundings, any more than coconuts will grow in Detroit.

Choosing Our Spiritual Environment

The error of most spiritual life is seeking to live as a Christian without the proper environment. Many Christians in our country assume that "the American way" is not at odds with the Christian lifestyle. They think that our cultural environment is "friendly" to the soul. Because American know-how has produced the richest nation on earth, we assume that our materialistic lifestyle is somehow synonymous with success, and thus with being first-class human beings.

In reality, the basic American lifestyle and its primary philosophy are detrimental to soul life. This is demonstrated by the type of Christianity we see today. Here the church establishment is marked by competition and division. Its membership is plagued by soul weakness and sin, rather than by holiness and righteousness. We emphasize being born "from above," born again, but we give a low priority to providing a suitable environment for growth. Something is wrong!

Henry Drummond, in *Natural Law in the Spiritual World*, reminds us that "Inner examination is good, but useless if we do not examine our outer environment. To bewail our weakness is right, but it is not remedial."

Our spiritual genes—our life forces—come from God, our Father, and we have no choice about this. But we can choose our inner and outer spiritual environment.

The church's job is to provide a positive general environment for the soul and encourage its members to make the right choices as to specifics in the world's environmental influences. And the Holy Spirit will *help* us choose the proper environment! Recently "Jane," a teenager from our church, was in a store shopping with some of her friends. Suddenly she was very uncomfortable with the loud rock music being played. She thought, *This kind of music has never bothered me before. Maybe the Lord is trying to tell me something.*

Right then and there "Jane" asked him what he wanted her to do. He said, "Just tell your friends you'll wait outside for them." Since "Jane" didn't want to act like a goody-two-shoes in front of her friends, the Lord provided a simple way to solve her dilemma.

Have you had a similar experience? If so, the Holy Spirit was helping you choose the proper environment for your soul.

Question:
Dr. Peale,
your practical suggestions and exercises
have helped me in troubled times.
In good times, however,
I have a tendency
to forget the faith and power.
Do you have any suggestions
for spiritual exercises
for approaching God
and obtaining guidance
when times are good?

Answer:
The best prescription
against spiritual complacency
is to develop the discipline
of having a daily quiet time.
Prayer is conversing with God,
spending time with Him,
getting to know Him
as you would any friend.
In fact,
if you have a consistent prayer time
during the smooth periods of life,
you will have developed
a strong support base to help you
through the difficulties.

Norman Vincent Peale and
Ruth Stafford Peale

10

Discipline #1
Knowing and Loving God

> God alone can make us godly
> and keep us that way.

It follows that, to become godly, we need to spend time alone with God. For this, there is no substitute. It was said of the early disciples, "They took knowledge of them that they had been with Jesus," not that they were talented, educated, or dynamic. So it must be said of us.

The Alchemy of Influence

As we spend quality time with God, we will love him more and will increasingly be transformed to be like him. The alchemy of influence always works. We become like those with whom we habitually hang around and have fellowship. If you are not willing to be intimate with God, forget ever becoming godly. You can be "religious" (by the world's definition) without spending time with him, but not godly.

Getting to First Base

Today's church has forgotten (or never really knew) *where* the first base of the Christian life lies and even *what* it is.

Suppose the scribe who came to Jesus would have asked him, "What is first base?" meaning what is the most important rule for a life.

Jesus told us about our first base when he answered that question with a very clear and definite: "'. . . YOU SHALL LOVE THE LORD YOUR GOD WITH ALL YOUR HEART, AND WITH ALL YOUR SOUL, AND WITH ALL YOUR MIND, AND WITH ALL YOUR STRENGTH'" (Mark 12:30).

How do we do this? We learn to love God like we learn to love any other person: by getting to know him. John said, "Beloved, let us love one another, for love is from God; and everyone who loves is born of God and knows God. *The one who does not love does not know God,* for God is love" (1 John 4:7–8, italics mine).

Because God *is* love, there is something unique about the first base of Christian life. Remember what was said in chapter 9 about our cause-and-effect world and choosing the proper environment for the health of our soul? Well, love is special in that it is *both* cause and effect. Faith, praise, and hope are basic spiritual attitudes, and they are spontaneously caused by love. But human love itself is an effect, the result of God's love for us.

Seeking → Knowing → Loving

The depth of love in any relationship is in direct proportion to the knowledge people have of each other, the degree of their intimacy. So, if I want the effect of loving God, I must seek to know him. If I seek him (cause), he has promised that I will get to know him (effect) and therefore love him. "Seeking is a personal, deliberate act. It is possible to find something accidentally, but you can't seek accidentally," says Richard Champion.

> And without faith it is impossible to please Him, for he who comes to God must believe that He is, and that He is a rewarder of those who seek Him (Heb. 11:6).

> [Thus says the Lord:] "And you will seek Me and find Me, when you search for Me with all your heart" (Jer. 29:13).

> [The Lord said through Moses:] "But from there you will seek the LORD your God, and you will find Him if you search for Him with all your heart and all your soul" (Deut. 4:29).

This should not seem strange to any of us. This is the way I came to love my wife. As I sought her company and interacted with her on dates, I got to know her. Then love just happened, and it continues to happen in an ever-increasing way.

The same is true with God, who so desires intimacy with us that he has already come to live within us. He cannot get any closer than that, but if we want to activate our intimacy with God, we must create space for him in our daily lives.

You say your schedule is already pretty full? Sure, so is mine. The solution (assuming that you are serious about creating space for God) is to get rid of something you are already doing—and it can't be sleep!

A Space-Making Guide

Let me share with you some very practical suggestions about creating time/space for God in your life.

It needs to be quality space—time when you are doing nothing but giving your individual attention to God and to him alone.

It needs to be when you are at your best physically and mentally. For this reason, most people create time/space in the morning, not in the evening when they are tired and least alert. However, if you are a "night person," spend time with him in the evening.

It needs to be long enough and unhurried. I suggest you plan *at least* one-half hour. God is surely worth as much time as a TV commentator, who gives thirty minutes of daily news, most of it irrelevant to us. This is not a time when you can be rushed or try to rush God. God wants to live with his people. He said to Moses, "And let them construct a sanctuary for Me, that I may dwell among them" (Exod. 25:8).

It needs to be a regular time, preferably daily. Once a week might be better than nothing, but only a little bit better. This would be like dieting one day a week and would have very little effect. Jesus gave the disciples a model prayer, one phrase of which says, "Give us this day our *daily* bread." He was showing us the most basic cycle of life. We are creatures of habit, and our strongest habits are those we do daily. A series of good habits makes up a good lifestyle. Spending time with God needs to become so habitual that when something keeps us from it, we really miss it.

It needs to be relevant time. We do not continue anything for very long if it is not pertinent to our life. A matter has purpose when it brings change that I can see and detect over a period of time. A matter is meaningful when it brings enjoyment. It is almost impossible to keep doing things for an extended time if they are boring and seemingly useless.

Encountering God

If you encounter God, it cannot help but be relevant to your life and healthy for your soul. The spiritual exercises that follow are based on these assumptions:

1. God the Father and Christ the Lord desire fellowship and communication with us—the communication of father with child, lover with beloved, friend with friend.
2. Through the Holy Spirit, God is present in each of us, ready for communication. Adrian Rogers asks, "Where on earth does God live?" The answer is always the same. "In us."
3. God will communicate with us on our level. As a father speaks with his children according to where they are mentally and emotionally, so God does with us.
4. It is easy to commune with God if we are willing to do it *his* way. Listen to Jesus' promise to his disciples: "And I will ask the Father, and He will give you another Helper, that He may be with you forever; that is the Spirit of truth . . . [and] you know Him because He abides with you, and will be in you. I will not leave you as orphans; I will come to you" (John 14:16–18).

Method One: Meditation on Scripture

The Scriptures were never intended to be read for content alone. They were to be a springboard for getting to know God. In the Bible we find:

Love letters from God, calling us to him
A map to guide us into his presence
A recipe to help us recognize his purposes
Clues to the ultimate treasure: God himself

There are many valid approaches to Scripture, but whichever one you take, make sure it is leading you closer to God. But always beware of seeking to analyze God. Instead, try to *know* him intimately and meaningfully. For instance, a psychiatrist knows all kinds of technical facts about his women patients but if he has never had a meaningful love relationship with a woman he has missed an important part of God's plan for man.

Many people think they have a systematic approach, a way to study God. They may know some truths about him, yet not really know him because they have no relationship with him.

You might read the Bible as a book, study its language or topics, memorize relevant verses, or analyze its themes—and all these approaches are useful. But I would like to suggest an approach that I call "meditation by journaling." Here you sit at Jesus' feet and let the Holy Spirit who lives in you explain the Scriptures as authored by the Father. Not only will he explain and interpret, but he will make them applicable to your life. Quite simply, journaling is writing down God's communications with you.

Reasons for Journaling. Before we go over a simple way to do this, I'll share some reasons why this method works so well as a way to know God. First, it slows down the mind. If you are going to write out the communication, your thoughts must slow down to your writing speed. Since this also keeps your mind from wandering, you concentrate on God and what he is saying to you.

Second, journaling helps fulfill "the law of developed consciousness." We develop consciousness of anything by giving expression to our sensory information. Writing down your impressions of what God is saying is one way of giving expression to the thoughts he places in your mind. You will find it easier and easier to do this because you will become more sensitive to the impressions.

Third, the faintest ink is better than the strongest memory. When you write down God's communication, you can accurately review it at a time when it might be more significant.

The Way of Journaling. If you have followed my soul-care guidelines so far, you have created space/time for God in your daily schedule—a definite meeting time. You also need a particular place where you meet with him alone, free from interruptions. It should be a comfortable place, and it is best not to have anyone else in the room at the time. This is one reason why early in the morning is better for most people, unless you have a very large house. If you are a mother with small children, their nap time might be suitable, but take the telephone off the hook! Have the necessary equipment ready: a Bible, a notebook, and a pencil or pen.

Here is a suggested procedure to follow at first (when you are comfortable in this you will develop your own style):

Step 1: In your notebook, write a love note to God, a thank-you letter. Here's one of mine: "Heavenly Father, Thank you for rest last night, for another day, for that cup of coffee, for the shower and clean clothes. I look forward to this time with you. Thanks so much. I love you!"

In doing this I have (a) set my mind on God; (b) articulated my thoughts by writing them out; and (c) created an attitude of gratitude by giving specific thanks to God. I have recognized him as the source of all good things, entering "His gates with thanksgiving," and "His courts with praise" (Ps. 100:4).

Step 2: Open your Bible to where you stopped the day

before. Write out the next unit of thought from the Scriptures. It might be one or more verses or even part of a verse, but it ought to be a unit of thought.

After writing out the Scripture, you pray (or write out): "Heavenly Father, please tell me what I need to know right now from this Scripture." Then take your pen and write down the thoughts that the Holy Spirit places in your mind about that Scripture. Listen to God!

This is a condensed excerpt from my journaling on Psalm 10: "Why dost Thou stand afar off, O LORD? Why dost Thou hide Thyself in times of trouble" (v. 1).

> *You wonder why I don't come to you when you are in trouble? . . . Why I don't come to your aid? Why I am still and silent? It is not because I do not see or do not care. It is because I will not be used by you. . . . So often the only reason you want me is to get you away from your problems and then you go on your own way until you need me again. When you get in this condition I stop acting, not because I do not care, but because I do care.*
>
> *I know your selfishness, your desire for your own good. But your own success is a sure way to destroy yourself. If I were to come to you as a servant . . . you would use me as a servant.*
>
> *I love you too much for this. I will remain silent toward you . . . till you want me for what I am, GOD, so you can worship me . . . follow me . . . obey me. All the preaching and all the praying will not bring me. When you earnestly seek me for myself . . . I will come.*

As you practice journaling and become more mature, you will usually get stronger impressions. It is quite possible for the Holy Spirit to say sometimes, "There is nothing here for you now." If he says this, I would write it down and go to the next unit of thought.

It is easier for most people to go through one book at a time. (For the first few years I suggest that you stay in the New Testament, the "new covenant.") You will move very slowly through the Scriptures this way, but the amount of Scripture read is not the issue. The point is how much of its truth is written in your heart and how much closer you are to God.

My Testimony. In forty years of voluntary Bible reading and study, this method has been the most profitable for me. And I enjoy the Scriptures as never before. They are stepping-stones into the Lord's presence. Now the Holy Spirit applies and personalizes the Scriptures for me.

As I've journaled, the Holy Spirit has taken obscure and difficult Bible passages and given them new meaning in my life and experience. Journaling has made it increasingly easier to hear from my God and Father, my Lord and Savior.

Method Two: Journaling in Prayer

Prayer, of course, is another and perhaps more frequently used way of encountering God—getting to know him and love him on an intimate level, which is the general aim of what I have called Discipline #1. Unfortunately, prayer is often misused or, rather, misunderstood as to its purpose.

All prayer is essentially a way of communicating with God. It is not merely presenting a "wish list" to him (the way many of us tend to use it). To be most effective, all prayer should begin with an expression of our praise, thanksgiving, and obedience. Then it is important that we open ourselves to what *he* has to say. That includes allowing him to direct what we will request of him. God knows our needs better than we do. When we subordinate our will and desires to what he has in mind

for us, he will grant our petitions, although not always
in the manner we think he should.

For several years one of my friends has had one
heartache and trial after the other. In prayer he was talking over the difficulties with the Lord. He asked, "God,
why have you allowed all this to happen to me?" The
answer he got humbled my friend and changed his
focus. God reminded him:

> You know too much of the situation,
> but too little of me.
> I'm omnipotent, almighty, ruler of the universe.
> Is anything too great for me?
> My life, my power, my purposes
> are revealed in tough situations like yours.
> **You know too much of the situation,**
> **but too little of me.**

My friend's view was changed immediately. Now his
focus is on God rather than on the situation.

This two-way process is illustrated in the diagram
below. Notice that this is a dynamic happening, with
the Triune God—Father, Son, and Holy Spirit—working
within our spiritual being to initiate and form our
prayer and then bring about intercession for the well-
being of the soul.

The journaling method can also be used for prayer, and I have found this very effective for opening the door of communication with God. As with meditation on Scripture, you need quiet, uninterrupted time and space—and a notebook. I suggest these steps for an effective prayer time:

Step 1: Give God thanks for the person or subject in your thoughts. *Example:* "Heavenly Father, I thank you for my son, John. I am grateful for his sweet disposition."

Step 2: Ask the Father how you should pray, or ask what his will is concerning the matter before you. *Example:* "Heavenly Father, how can I pray for my son John today?"

Step 3: Write out the answer he gives you. *Example:* "Peter, John needs encouragement from you today. Write him a letter and tell him how you love him."

An Overview

Soul-care Discipline #1 is spending intimate time with God so that you get to know and love him more deeply. There is no way to pass this up if you desire a healthy soul.

There are many good books encouraging and giving instruction on both Scripture meditation and prayer. You will want to read these from time to time to learn how others have been enriched by communicating with our Lord.

I am shedding pride. . . .
I shall ask into my shell
only those friends
with whom I can be completely honest.
I find I am shedding hypocrisy
in human relationships.
What a rest that will be.
The most exhausting thing in life,
I have discovered,
is being insecure.
That is why
so much of social life is exhausting;
one is wearing a mask.
I have shed my mask.

Anne Morrow Lindbergh
Gift from the Sea

11

Discipline #2
Loving and Being Loved Through Fellowship

Recie Young, Greg Charles, Randy Hudgins, Dennis Filler, Randy Coleman, Bob Nickerson, Ray Lockridge, Mark Glenn. What do these men have in common with each other and with me, Peter Lord?

First, let me say, these are true citizens of the kingdom of God. You have probably never heard of them before and never will again. But they are important to me and extremely important to God our Father. You see, they are the here-and-now people in my life and ministry. They are people I interact with on a regular basis: my neighbors, my near ones. I receive the grace of God through these men and share his grace with them.

What do they have in common by the world's reckoning? Not much. They vary in age (from 21 to 35), vocation (engineers, funeral director, artist, student, salesman, musician, gardener), family background (good families, bad families, no families), cultural background (from all over America), lifestyle (divorced, successful, poor, various values).

So what do they have in common? From God's viewpoint, everything. They are children of his family, living in the same spiritual room of God's big house right now. This small group meets at my house every Monday night. Other times, we often get together socially and spiritually. We are bound together in a small group to watchcare, edify, encourage, and build each other up in our love for God. We are actually a church, an important but very small part of the body of Christ. The main thrust of our group is nurture, so we may grow to spiritual manhood.

A Team Sport

In my experience as a pastor, individuals do not grow to spiritual maturity without teamwork—intimate interaction of some form within a small group, for the purpose of a shared goal: soul care.

In individual sports, such as tennis, track, or swimming, athletes can win solely on their own merit, ability, strength, and determination. This is not true in team sports like football, baseball, hockey, basketball. One person cannot win alone, no matter how great he or she is.

When I was starting out, no one ever told me that Christianity is and always will be a team sport. I thought it was something you could do alone if you chose to. That is, you could be a winner as a Christian without being in dynamic, intimate relationships with others of like purpose.

In a team sport, a cooperative effort is needed to score points. That makes everybody important. Even though fans glorify the superstars in such sports, the stars know that to win they need the whole team. A great running back in football needs the blocking linemen, or he would never make it to the end zone.

To a large degree, people in our part of the world do not seem to know about Christian teamwork. Many Christians think the most important people are the superstars. Do you realize your great importance to the kingdom and to God? Or do you feel insignificant, and so act as if you cannot make a difference?

Here's a cartoon to illustrate the principle. Let's assume that it represents several people on the way to Christian maturity. There's a roadblock, a crisis (there are always several on the Christian walk). You may have already guessed the solution, but if not, I'll show you later how teamwork solves the problem.

"We" = Fellowship

In Christianity, we cannot win alone. We need others, and others need us. That translates into fellowship. The Bible doesn't portray solo Christians. It points out teams like Paul, Silas, and Timothy. Most of the original-language verbs in the Bible referring to the saints are in second-person plural: "you all," not "you." Such is true when it says, "You are the temple of the living God." Second-person plural means that *together* we are the body of Christ; we are not to function as isolated individuals.

During a conference in California, friends stayed at the Mount Hermon Conference Center in the mountains outside Santa Cruz. Surrounded by the giant sequoias, they watched a bulldozer working right outside their dining room window. Patiently the noisy machine scraped and scooped until it exposed the entire root system of the trees rimming the excavation site. My friends wondered how such puny shallow roots could keep these giants from toppling during winds and storms.

Later that day they visited a nearby park. Walking in the deep shadows cast by the immense sequoias, they gazed up at these tall trees until their necks ached. Then they asked the park guide how the shallow root system supported such mass and height. He explained that the trees grow in a circle. Their roots intertwined and clustered directly beneath the earth's surface, enabling them to stand and survive nature's destructive forces together.

Life is often a bulldozer. You can choose to be a loner or instead be like the sequoia, its roots intertwined with others, growing in a group. We all need family, friends, and other small groups to survive and grow to be all God intended us to be. God created us to reinforce, sustain, and nurture each other. This is the way we survive the destructive forces loose in our environment, the world.

How did we get where we are—private individuals operating without real community? The rugged individualism of the American cultural history influences our thinking. Even as we read the Bible we think "I," while the Bible means "we."

You can't have a healthy soul or serve God effectively as an individual until you are on a team. People need you in a dynamic relationship, and you need them.

Christians will never move to spiritual maturity except in a unit. This is the reason I'm in this small group and you should be in one, too.

How We Do

"What do you do in your small group?" This is the first question most people ask, but it is not the most important one. The better question focuses on *how*, not *what* we do. First off, we are NOT specifically a Bible study group, a prayer group, a share group, or a ministry group. We are a *church*, doing all of these and more. But our relationships are those of family, not a schoolroom or job or ministry team, even though all these dynamics can and do take place.

There are basically two types of small groups: *nurture groups*, whose main purpose is development; and *ministry groups*, whose members are together for spiritual guidance and care (we never come to the place where we do *not* need nurture and care).

Participation

This first how-we-do means that everybody takes an active part. Our group meeting is not a performance by a leader, where the others are mere spectators. The "leader" of our group is not a boss. He is more a moderator, one who knows he is both servant and facilitator to the others, deferring to them and encouraging their input. We are all learning that the same Jesus Christ lives in us as in Jamie Buckingham, Adrian Rogers, or Robert Schuller. Each of us realizes that even though his contribution may be different from another's, it is as important and significant to the body of Christ. Everyone in the Christian fellowship is a full team member. This is hard to believe if you get your values from today's superstar culture.

In 1 Corinthians 12:22–24, Paul strongly emphasizes this truth: In fact, to illustrate the idea of "differences" further, compare the two versions below—each making the same point uniquely:

The Living Bible:
And some of the parts that seem weakest and least important are really the most necessary. Yes, we are especially glad to have some parts that seem rather odd! And we carefully protect from the eyes of others those parts that should not be seen, while of course the parts that may be seen do not require this special care. So God has put the body together in such a way that extra honor and care are given to those parts that might otherwise seem less important.

The New Testament in Modern English (J. B. Phillips Edition):
On the contrary, those parts of the body which seem to have less strength are more essential to health; and to those parts of the body which seem to us to be less admirable we have to allow the highest honor of function. The parts which do not look beautiful have a deeper beauty in the work they do, while the parts which look beautiful may not be at all essential to life! But God has harmonized the whole body by giving importance of function to the parts which lack apparent importance, that the body should work together as a whole with all the members in sympathetic relationship with one another.

Honesty

The second how-we-do frees and encourages everybody to be honest about where he is, what he feels, what he thinks.

It is easy to be honest about the good we do, the victories we win, our answered prayers and revelation received. But it is essential that we also be honest about:

> defeats we experience
> dark valleys we go through
> perplexities and disappointments we have
> despair we feel
> weakness and failures we are facing
> temptations we are experiencing
> needs we are suffering

It is in our down times that we need each other the most. When we are down, it is easy for the enemy to get to us.

We are not honest if we only talk about the good things, the up moments. We are dishonest hypocrites when we pretend, wear masks, act as though all is simply wonderful when it is not.

One night, for example, one of the members came to the group down and discouraged. As we got the meeting started, he said, "Wait. If I don't say what I need to say now, I will probably not do it. This past week I failed. I slipped back into drugs. I need help."

We junked the planned program and spent the first half-hour ministering to him. Assuring him of our love, we prayed for him. Some in the group shared similar experiences and God's faithfulness to them in their failures. From time to time others have shared temptations of lust, hate, fear, pride, failures with drugs, anger, fear, and so on.

In a group, an absolute formula for failure begins with PARTIAL HONESTY → goes to NO REAL SHARING → this results in NO HONESTY → we progress to NO FELLOWSHIP → everyone is PLAY-ACTING → ending with HYPOCRISY.

Within our small-group context, however, a person can be nurtured beyond the denial and defense mechanisms that hinder honesty in any relationship and block one's personal growth.

"Denial" sounds technical; but, simply put, we all have the uncanny tendency to avoid honestly looking at a problem in our lives—family, job, marriage, whatever—until the problem severely damages us in some way. We can actually look at a particular problem and deny that it has anything to do with us. Of course, if we refuse to acknowledge the existence of a problem, the status quo can be maintained. We don't have to do anything! But the problem is unsolved, and our pain remains hidden, growing beneath the surface of our consciousness until it becomes excruciating.

Let me illustrate "denial" with a short parable. At Centerville High, every student had to have a physical examination to play sports. During this exam, the doctor pushed on Fred Fullback's abdomen, causing tremendous pain. (Fred, we might add, had already been experiencing periodic minor bouts of abdominal pain, which he had been ignoring.) The doctor explained that Fred had appendicitis, requiring immediate surgery. Fred got very angry and said *he* didn't have a problem, since he was doing okay until the doctor poked and prodded him. Therefore, the doctor had the problem—and Fred didn't want him pushing on him like that again!

Now let me explain what I mean by "defense mechanism," which is also a behavior (or system of behaviors) we perform to avoid facing and dealing with our problems. In the example above, Fred would refuse to have the exam. If the coach insisted on his seeing the doctor like everyone else on the team (and therefore being prodded), Fred would simply drop out of sports altogether, though he loved playing football. All this so he wouldn't have to accept the fact that he had a problem with his appendix! (And we know that problem didn't go away by itself.)

Honesty is perhaps the hardest how-we-do in the

small group because of the training and practice we have had in wearing masks. As we pass this barrier (and to the degree we pass it), we enter into intimacy, without which real love through fellowship is impossible.

Sharing and Caring

Recently, one member shared the problems of his small business and his desperate need for immediate cash. He was completely broke, with not even enough money for gas. Yes, we all prayed together, but we also gave him some hard American dollars. We shared our abundance to meet his deficit.

Sharing with each other some of what God has given to us is an important small-group concept. What we share ranges from money to selfless agape love. The apostle John spells this out:

> We know love by this, that He laid down His life for us; and we ought to lay down our lives for the brethren. But whoever has the world's goods, and beholds his brother in need and closes his heart against him, how does the love of God abide in him? (1 John 3:16–17).

Agape love is the sharing of all things with others according to their need. This includes money, time, talent, and anything else we have.

We first show we care by taking time to know each other intimately. When we have spent time listening, we can share easily and fully our love, encouragement, wisdom, forgiveness, money, skills, revelation—and more.

Developing Christ-Consciousness

It is one thing for Christ to dwell in us. It is quite another thing for us to be fully aware of his presence. Since conscious awareness of anything is a trainable skill, another how-we-do in our group focuses on developing Christ-consciousness.

Each member shares some evidence of Christ's presence in his life during the past week. Recalling and sharing reinforce our perceptions of any experience, so that the more we are able to share evidence of Christ's presence, the more we will be conscious of him.

One cannot live the Christian life by a system of commandments, but only by a living, vital relationship with Christ. Regular spiritual exercises (such as in the preceding chapter) often reveal the indwelling Christ in a startling new way, sparking a spontaneous, easy, and ongoing recognition of his presence.

Another learning technique we encourage is inviting Christ into a particular situation and then asking him what he would have us do or say. For myself, I set personal disciplines. Of course, before I do anything *important*, I will commit it to the Lord and see if he has any instruction. But even before going out to a party or dinner, I will ask Christ to quicken me to any way I can be a blessing to others in his behalf. What I am really after is the development of a habit where I spontaneously speak and act according to my consciousness of Christ's presence in me.

What We Do

Small groups are as different as the people in them. So there are many ways to accomplish the how-we-do purposes cited above. Each group has its own genetic code. (Don't try to be a clone.) Another point is that nothing about our group is rigidly ordered. We are always open to the wind of the Holy Spirit to guide and change.

The framework for our group meeting normally includes time for sharing, praying, learning, worshiping, and ministry. Although our meeting time is roughly blocked out into four segments, each of those functions overlaps and flows into the others.

Thanksgiving

First we give thanks, each thanking God for blessings of the past. This is specific and relative to where we are in our present life. Giving thanks accomplishes three purposes. It focuses our attention on God; it pleases God; and it creates a grateful atmosphere so that we more easily love each other.

Sharing

Next we share "Last Week's Jesus." Each person relates a situation in the past seven days wherein he became conscious of the indwelling Christ and released him to be Lord in his life. For example, one member once shared how Christ helped him through a difficult relationship problem when a fellow worker falsely accused him of wrongdoing.

What we try to share doesn't need to be sensational, because we are not trying to outdo each other. The reasons for this sharing are to make Christ current, to get us more and more conscious of the indwelling Christ, and to demonstrate the presence and interest of Christ in *all* of life's situations: home, work, social, and play.

Study and Application

Bible study is not a major part of our time. Like the average person, we know more than we are putting into practice now, so our emphasis is on applying the truth we know. We are trying to build biblical truth into our lifestyles so we can live it naturally and spontaneously. Most of our studies relate to the development of the inner life, such as hearing God, gaining a good conscience, abiding in Christ, and having true faith. After a truth is presented, we have a shared time of application. Paul's warning to the Corinthian church, "Knowledge makes arrogant, but love edifies" (1 Cor. 8:1), is especially relevant here.

Facts and study aids are easy to get today. For not much money you can buy or rent a tape of a dynamic speaker on any subject, and there are numerous books on faith-related topics. Remember, though, that knowledge brings with it pride. But love is truth in action.

Praise, Worship, and Ministry

Consciously giving God praise and trust, we next move into worship. As we do this, an individual may reveal a specific need. Then we stop and ask our Father how to meet this need. We pray until the individual gets peace. Then we continue our praise.

We look for opportunities to have "feast days," at our meetings, celebrating birthdays, marriages, promotions, and other important events. And our interaction continues during the week. This week, for example, I helped Greg with a plumbing problem; Recie chauffeured me to the airport; Mark and Ray had a meal together; and so on. Such small relationship-building events help bond people together in Christ. I am a sixty-year-old professional in the church, a pastor all my adult life, yet weekly these men minister grace, love, and help to me. Some evenings I begin the meeting tired and worn out. At the end of our time together, I am exhilarated and full of God's grace.

Over the years, I have been nurtured in several small-group settings. The first fellowship group of which I was a part met every Friday morning for two years and was formed out of our shared desire to go more deeply into Christ. At first, we were not sure how to go about this, but the Holy Spirit showed us the way. We no longer meet regularly, but through the years the members have been major contributors to church life, many in leadership positions.

For several years, my wife and I once met every Sunday evening with seven other couples. Here, our bonds of congeniality and our marriages were strengthened by our growing knowledge and experience of Christ. Our friendships continue to this day.

I currently participate in a small group that consists of the elders of our church (currently nine). We are bound together by common interests and burdens: the responsibility of being God's servants to a large number of people. Our goal is to enrich our church work through a mutual support system. These men have been my counselors (and critics, since they know my weaknesses as well as my strengths!) in many situations, and I believe the action has been reciprocal.

In addition, there is the group of single men I have already described. Many of these men have not only become more firmly established in partnership with God but have married and graduated to a group for couples. Meeting with these younger Christians has brought me down from the ivory tower of preaching into the practicalities of everyday life.

I have pastored the same church for the past twenty-four years and can say without hesitation that the small-group experience is the most rewarding and lasting ministry I have had during this time. The separate groups I have belonged to represent a broad spectrum of people and purposes, but all in their own way have been powerful examples of what I call Discipline #2 for soul care—loving through fellowship.

The Tie That Binds Forever

Let's flip back to the cartoon at the beginning of this chapter, a picture of people tied together in Christ and going through life together. Through the power of the cross, here's how victory over crisis is won:

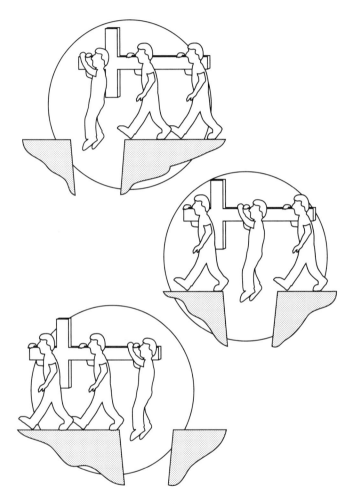

If you are the middle man, can you name at least two others to whom you are tied in a covenant way and who will carry you over the chasm?

Two are better than one because they have a good return for their labor. For if either of them falls, the one will lift up his companion. But woe to the one who falls when there is not another to lift him up. . . . And if one can overpower him who is alone, two can resist him. A cord of three strands is not quickly torn apart (Eccles. 4:9–10, 12).

For me, the small-group setting provides the opportunity to develop a deeper relationship with the Lord, as he works within and through our circle of fellowship. It is a context for genuine and openly expressed agape love—the selfless love epitomized by Jesus Christ.

Of course, as in any give-and-take relationship (where *trust* is required), the deeper the intimacy level, the deeper the risks to our prideful, worldly selves. But the rewards of this type of soul care are immeasurable. Bound together by the ties of Christian love, you, too, can discover new truths about yourself, find nurturance for your spiritual growth, and store renewed strength for the tough spots, present and future.

There will always be a few people who are physically or emotionally unable to meet with a small group of people. Does this mean that they will not be able to develop their soul to its fullest potential? No. God makes provisions for such exceptions. For those who cannot participate in a group setting, I suggest trying to get together with one other Christian as often as possible for sharing and praying. Or perhaps, a small Sunday school class may be an answer for you. Be comforted. If you do all you can, God will not fail to do all he can in you and through you.

Remember, the problem is not with those who *cannot*, it is with those who *will not*.

A French Fable

Once upon a time, a king had a faithful servant who was so hard working he was known throughout the kingdom. One day the servant took some rare time off and left the castle for a walk in the woods. Deep in the forest he blundered into a little glen where he saw a genie, sitting on a rock and holding a lamp in his hands.

"Good day, most faithful servant," the genie said. "I know of your fine reputation and I've been waiting for you. You've been a hard worker all your life, and now it's your turn for pleasure. With this magic lamp I can grant you one wish. Decide very carefully, because I can only grant you one wish," the genie warned.

Without hesitation the servant responded, "I don't want to serve anymore. From now on I want servants of my own. I will be the one ordering people around. And they'll do everything for me."

Sure enough, when the man got back to the castle, the guard opened the door for him. Servants rushed to cook his food, wash his dishes, and press his clothes. He no longer had to work. Servants did everything for him, including serving his former master, the king.

At first, the novelty of the experience delighted the man, but soon it got annoying. After three months, he couldn't stand it any longer.

Dashing to the woods, the man searched until he found the genie. He said, "I've found out that I don't like to be idle and have others serve me. I'd like my old job back—once again to be servant of the kingdom."

The genie answered, "I'm so sorry. Remember, I only had the power to grant you one wish, and so I can't help you."

The man said, "But you don't understand. I've discovered that serving others is far better than having others do things for me. You must help me. I'd rather be in hell than not be able to serve others."

The genie said sorrowfully, "My friend, where do you think you have been for the last ninety days?"

12

Discipline #3
Loving Through Service

All living organisms must maintain a balance between intake and outgo if they are to remain healthy. When we try to put out more than we have taken in, we exhaust our available resources, whether physical, financial, mental, or spiritual. When energy on any level is depleted, we say a person is suffering burnout.

On the other hand, if our input greatly exceeds our output, there is an overload and we can become stagnated, complacent, even parasitical. For a physically fit body and a sound mind, we must *use* what we have both appropriately and in full measure.

The same principle applies to the spiritual realm. Proper soul care requires that we must balance our spiritual intake with visible outgo. That basically means making our soul's energy accessible to others in need.

Just how available are *you* for service and ministry to

others? The intake of God's grace must be exercised in service to prevent the apathy, indifference, and other evils so common in the church that they become acceptable as normal. Today, highly trained ministers are paid to perform the work of the church, and the typical church member has become a spectator at the professional's performance. But there is no substitute for selfless service to others for our soul's health and growth.

What Is Ministry?

What does the word *ministry* mean to you? What picture comes to your mind? Witnessing to a non-Christian? Teaching a Sunday-school lesson? Taking a mission trip? Singing a solo in the choir?

If so, cancel those ideas for now. Yes, these can be channels of legitimate ministry, but they are probably not practical for the majority of us. Ministry is service, which means serving—giving yourself for the welfare of another person you have no reason to care about other than God's love.

Whatever way you serve, if it is Christian service it will involve these four elements:

1. *It will take quality time.* This requires that you be truly *present* in what you are doing. Serving that builds your soul is not the kind you can pay other people to do. Service is like physical exercise in that no one can do it for you.

2. *You will be giving part of yourself during that time.*

Sometimes it is listening to someone who needs to talk.

Sometimes it is giving your companionship to someone who is lonely.

Sometimes it requires your energy, as in house cleaning.

Sometimes it is using a special talent or ability.

Sometimes it is speaking words of encouragement, comfort, or edification.

3. *It is expending your life for someone with a genuine need.* It may be a need on any level: body, soul, spirit, social, or material, but it is a legitimate need. Because it is easier to do, we often give ourselves to people without need. This is what is meant in Luke 14:12–14: "And He [Jesus] also went on to say to the one who had invited Him, 'When you give a luncheon or a dinner, do not invite your friends or your brothers or your relatives or rich neighbors, lest they also invite you in return, and repayment come to you. But when you give a reception, invite the poor, the crippled, the lame, the blind, and you will be blessed, since they do not have the means to repay you; for you will be repaid at the resurrection.'"

4. *It is given in the name of Christ and because of his love:*

> If I speak with the tongues of men and of angels, but do not have love, I have become a noisy gong or a clanging cymbal. And if I have the gift of prophecy, and know all mysteries and all knowledge; and if I have all faith, so as to remove mountains, but do not have love, I am nothing. And if I give all my possessions to feed the poor, and if I deliver my body to be burned, but do not have love, it profits me nothing (1 Cor. 13:1–3).

Simplicity in Serving

Often we do not serve because we have a wrong perception. We think of serving as big—complicated—all-

consuming—full time. So we have a mental block about
it.

The marks of true ministry are the opposite.
Christian service is simple, ordinary, at the moment it
is needed.

A fifteen-year-old girl's mom is in the hospital for
surgery. The girl needs to stay with someone for a couple of nights.

A bride's wedding-reception plans are falling apart.
She needs someone to bake four dozen cookies.

A widow has a flat tire in the church parking lot. She
needs someone to take care of it for her.

A hospice group advertises on local radio that they
need yarn and fabric scraps.

Whom Shall I Serve?

When people say to me, "I do not know anybody in
need," I recognize one of two things. They are not soul-
sensitive, or they are blind, if they cannot see need in a
world crammed full of needy people. That includes the
"world" within a few hundred yards of most of us and
the "world" of our weekly schedule.

Start where you are. Be a channel of God's love to
people within your easy reach in time and space. Here
are a few beginning guidelines:

1. Begin and concentrate on one needy person,
    asking God to lead you to him or her.
2. Begin with a person near you—in your neighbor-
    hood, your work force, your weekly flow of
    activity.
3. Here is a potential sampling: widows, orphans, the
    lonely, the depressed, the elderly or infirm, the
    handicapped.

Seek to minister to a person outside your *phileo*—your natural love flow (choose someone other than family and friends). *Agape* is love for somebody you would not ordinarily minister to except for Christ's sake.

Remember, you are not aiming to convert this person to your point of view, but only trying to serve in the name of Christ. Some of those to whom you minister will come to know Christ, but this is not your primary objective. Your immediate aim is to exercise your soul by giving yourself to another—loving through service.

Basic Ministry Tools

There are many tools we may use to minister to and serve other people. The two basic ones are "acceptance" and "encouragement."

Acceptance

To minister to another person I must accept that individual and communicate that acceptance to him or her. If I am going to minister to other people consistently and effectively, I must have a high A.Q. (Acceptance Quotient). People do not care how much you know, till they know how much you care.

There are many levels of A.Q. Since Jesus would have scored a perfect 100 while he was here on earth—living in a human body and with the same kind of people we live with—let us look at some aspects of his A.Q.

First, he communicated acceptance of all sorts of people. Thieves, prostitutes, the spiritually weak, everyone felt free to come to him. When we realize that this Holy One without sin welcomed all, we see it is possible for us to accept the unholy as primarily people in need—and let them know it.

All types of people felt accepted by Jesus, including

the downtrodden, the sick, the poor. Jesus was available to the very worst, as far as society was concerned. He was accused of "eating with the publicans and sinners." Since he was eating in their homes, it means he accepted their invitations and thus their company. He also graciously received society's elite—Nicodemus, the Pharisees, and the rich young ruler.

Above all, Jesus accepted people blinded by sin, those who disagreed with him, disappointed him, let him down, or criticized him. When we can accept only those who love us or who are like us, who do not harm us or who bless us, we do no more than people who do *not* know God. Jesus valued everyone and treated them accordingly.

Two often-neglected chapters in the Bible are Romans 14 and 15. In all of Paul's writing, the last part of each letter carried the practical outworking of the eloquent theology of the first part. Listen to the practical simplicity of accepting others, as found in those two chapters:

> Accept the weak in faith (those who do not agree with us).
>
> Accept them, though not to pass judgment.
>
> Accept them because God has done so.
>
> Do not judge your brother or hold him in contempt.
>
> Let us pursue peace and build up one another.
>
> We who are strong ought to bear the burdens of the weak.
>
> Let each of us please his neighbor for his good, to his edification.
>
> Accept one another as Christ has accepted us, to the glory of God.

How does Christ accept us? Just as we are—with all our faults, weaknesses, peculiarities, prejudices, bondages, and blunders. He doesn't say, "Change to be like me and *then* I will accept you." He knows that we could never do that. But he also knows that if we accept *his* acceptance of us, we will hang around him and be changed.

Seeing People with Christ's Eyes. How can we accept people like Christ did and still does? We can see them through his eyes. Here are some general suggestions that will help raise your A.Q.:

1. See everyone as a sinner for whom Christ died.
2. See every Christian as a family member and as chosen by God.
3. See every weakness, every objectionable characteristic, as a soul sickness that needs healing.
4. Remember that you, too, want to be accepted just as you are.

Acceptance in Action. Now that we know the general characteristics of a high A.Q., it may help to examine a few specifics in word and deed that can best convey to others that our feelings are genuine. Only then will there be a positive response to our efforts to minister to others.

1. *Reach out.* Go to those you perceive as needy or in pain. Christ *took* healing love to others. He did not wait until they came to him for help, and neither should we. Open the eye of your soul so that it sees the needs of people around you.

2. *Be persistent.* Approach people on a regular basis, but don't be surprised if they do not accept your initial expressions of interest. Those in need have been "used" so often by others that they may be suspicious of your motives at first. Consistency and warmth will break down the walls.

3. *Don't look for gratitude.* In particular, never try to get people to do something for *you* (e.g., come to church or join a Sunday school class). Invite, but don't pressure. Tangible signs that you are getting through will probably come in time. It is all too easy to want to win converts and not simply accept people for themselves.

4. *Invite them to share your home surroundings.* A dining room table provides a valuable setting for conveying acceptance, especially if your guests are served normal "family fare."

5. *Accentuate the positive.* Pay attention, as you minister to a person's needs, to his or her strong points. That way, you build up the other's self-esteem and motivation to move ahead.

6. *Encourage them to join you in activities you mutually enjoy.* Do together the things they are comfortable with. By finding out their interests, you can become all things to them.

7. *Never act shocked or judgmental about what they say or want to do.* Instead, sharpen your listening skills, remembering that communication is a two-way process. Help the other person discover solutions rather than imposing your ideas. Make suggestions when you feel they will be welcomed.

Encouragement

The second basic tool of an effective ministry is encouragement, the Greek word for which is *parakaleo.* It has the same word root as the title for Holy Spirit—the Paraclete—and is used to describe his work. A paraclete is one who comes alongside to help us on life's journey. The Holy Spirit lives in us, encouraging us and using us to encourage others. There is no greater, more needed, or helpful ministry than that of encourag-

ing another. When I encourage, I am joining the Holy
Spirit in his work here on earth.

There are two basic ideas for action that are implied
in the word *encouragement:* being alongside another,
and speaking words that help motivate another to go on.
More people are initially defeated in their Christian
walk by discouragement than any other one thing. In
fact, it is the evil one's favorite weapon.

You encourage other people exactly the same way you
are encouraged: by drawing on the Lord's strength.
"Blessed be the God and Father of our Lord Jesus Christ,
the Father of mercies and God of all comfort; who comforts us in all our affliction so that we may be able to
comfort those who are in any affliction with the comfort with which we ourselves are comforted by God
(2 Cor. 1:3–4).

There are many ways that God has encouraged me
through others over the years. For example, sincere
compliments of any kind, but especially those pertain-
ing to my spiritual life, my character, my lifestyle, or
my ministry, have often helped to buoy my spirits. I
once received a note from one of our church secretaries,
Jodi, telling me that I had "acted like Jesus" in a particular office situation. This was an encouraging word to me
in a somewhat difficult period.

Other times, someone has helped me get a different
perspective. When one is too close to a situation, or so
wounded by circumstances, one's focus is negative.
While I was going through crisis after crisis with one of
my children, a friend once said, "Your child really has a
good heart. He loves and respects you. Just hang in
there. He will make the right choices." That gave me a
renewed sense of hope. It has also been encouraging to
have people choosing to spend time with me for no

apparent reason. To be wanted for yourself and not for what you can do for someone is a very positive force in one's life.

We live in a day with a wide variety of communication tools:

1. *Notes.* Jo Moberg, a member of our fellowship, regularly encourages me with short to-the-point notes. Messages like these lift me up when I'm down, and they usually arrive at very strategic times.

2. *Phone Calls.* You can pick up the phone and call anyone, anywhere, in just a few minutes. A phone call is a useful, very personal channel, yet how few calls we make to encourage someone. (When I call people to do this, they sometimes ask, "Pastor, what do you want?" It is hard for some people to believe I'm not asking for anything, but just seeking to encourage them.)

3. *A Hug or a Squeeze.* We can convey our encouragement by touch or even by gesture. The bumper sticker that asks, "Have you hugged your kids today?" is communicating a very valid means of affirming God's love.

4. *Direct Encounters.* Always the best means of encouragement is face-to-face contact. Nothing can take the place of a word or action that says, "I care enough about you to give you my most valuable asset, my time." Sharing a meal is one effective way to do this, since we usually break bread only with those we really want to be with.

It is hard to go wrong encouraging another person. It is a basic ministry tool and scripturally endorsed:

> And we urge you, brethren, admonish the unruly, encourage the fainthearted, help the weak, be patient with all men (1 Thess. 5:14).

Comfort and strengthen your hearts in every good work and word (2 Thess. 2:17).

And let us consider how to stimulate one another to love and good deeds . . . encouraging one another; and all the more, as you see the day drawing near (Heb. 10:24–25).

PART 4

HEALING AN ACHING PAIN

Benjamin Franklin said,
"Those things that hurt instruct."

Most of us are not so wise. Fearing the pain involved, almost all of us, in varying degrees, attempt to avoid facing our problems. We procrastinate, hoping they will go away. Or we pretend they do not exist. We even take drugs to assist our self-delusions, hoping to deaden ourselves to the pain. This tendency to avoid emotional suffering by denying reality is the primary basis of all mental illness.

Carl Jung said,
"Neurosis is always a substitute for legitimate suffering."

"But the substitute itself ultimately becomes more painful than the legitimate suffering it was designed to avoid. . . . In any case, when we avoid the legitimate suffering that results from dealing with problems, we also avoid the growth that problems demand from us."

M. Scott Peck
The Road Less Traveled

13

The Nature of Soul Pain

Have you ever thanked God for pain? Why is pain valuable? What groups of people pray for their lost ability to feel pain? Interesting questions.

What Pain Is Saying

We are so body-conscious that we have developed vast systems to deal with physical pain. Large corporations and health-care professionals make millions by treating pain: pharmaceutical companies, drugstores, hospitals and clinics and their personnel.

Because we immediately respond to pain, we often pay heavy fees to treat it. Very few of us ignore even a toothache or severe cold. Instead, we go to the dentist or doctor or take a pill.

Yet, do we know how to treat soul pain? We take

aspirin for a headache, Pepto-Bismol for an upset stomach. But what do we do for emotional pains such as worry, anger, lust, or loneliness—signs that our soul is hurting?

Purposes of Pain

There are two basic purposes for pain: (1) protecting and directing; and (2) constructive.

Protective and Directive Purposes of Pain

Pain warns us of impending danger. Physical pain is witness to actual damage or trouble in a particular area of the body. It shouts, "Hey, something is wrong. Act." Moderate pain sensations warn me that a stove is hot and the situation will get worse if I don't immediately remove my hand. Even mild physical discomfort tells me that something is wrong with my body and that I should seek relief.

The soul, too, suffers pain. Learning how to recognize the warning signals of impending danger to our inner man is an important facet of soul care. And we should treat soul ache with the same concern we do physical discomfort. We must find out what's causing the soul's pain and correct it. Better still, we should learn how to prevent it.

Sometimes physical pain is specific and acute. My stomach hurts, my head aches, my back is sore, my chest is tight. Such pains indicate the need for immediate attention. Other times the warning is generalized and less urgent. Fatigue warns me to rest my body. Periodic heartburn may tell me to watch my diet and check out the reasons if the symptoms persist.

What is true of the body is also true of the soul. For

instance, we may experience the soul pain of guilt. We may feel this pain because we *are* guilty. When we have sinned, we need to deal with our transgression and the pain it causes the soul. Guilt is a warning, even if the guilt is imagined or exaggerated.

When we feel lonely, it is because God designed the soul to live in relationships. Loneliness warns us to seek the companionship of God and the church, his physical presence on earth. Fear, too, can overwhelm us when we allow it a place in our consciousness. Wrong thinking allows fear to grow, choking soul life.

These three—guilt, loneliness, and fear—are common soul pains, signals of an ailing soul. As with the body, there is a difference between persistent pain and momentary, fleeting pain that is specific to circumstances. Most momentary pain warns that something serious will happen if we don't act. Chronic pain indicates that something has already gone wrong, that damage is occurring and needs correction.

External Causes of Soul Pain. One dictionary defines pain as "a basic bodily sensation, induced by noxious stimuli, received by naked nerve endings, characterized by discomfort and typically leading to evasive action." Acute and sudden pain is often caused by a specific external force. If there is a stone in my shoe, I know it as soon as I take a step. In that case, I first react to the source—I remove the stone. Next, I repair any damage—I rub my foot or apply a Band-Aid if necessary. We refuse to tolerate the avoidable external conditions that cause us physical pain. We remove "noxious stimuli" if we can and then tend to the healing process.

We need to treat the soul with the same degree of care. Some soul pain is directly related to external conditions. For example, an unkind word or act by another, or a particular situation, can inflict the soul with pressures it was not designed to handle on its own. Our first reaction is usually to reject or eliminate the source of the pain. If possible, we avoid the offending person or circumstances in the future. If another person is the cause, we may then seek retaliation, mistakenly believing that this will bring healing to our soul.

But angry revenge leaves the soul unhealed! When the inner man is wounded, inner medication is needed—the healing that comes from God. First we must *confess* our negative feelings and also any part we may have played in inviting the injury. Is there something we have done that is partially to blame? God will direct our attention to our part in the problem.

Once we have confessed, God will forgive, reminding us that he totally loves and accepts us as we are. But we must forgive the one who has offended us if healing is to take place. The hurt may remain for a while, but forgiveness will restore the health of our soul, even if it does not completely restore the relationship to what it once was. Healing of the soul involves walking in the light of the Great Physician: "But if we walk in the light as He Himself is in the light, we have fellowship with one another, and the blood of Jesus His Son cleanses us from all sin" (1 John 1:7).

Internal Causes of Soul Pain. It is not always so easy to identify the source of inner aches. When our pain is generalized, the evil one is often at work—attacking us with bad thoughts and negative interpretations of circumstances. In that case, there is usually chronic and generalized soul pain, which is harder to deal with. It is possible to live in such pain for so long that we accept it as normal. Then we no longer recognize that healing is needed. Here are some examples:

1. *Loneliness, Feelings of Rejection.* These pains are related to the soul's need for fellowship, for communion and companionship with God and our fellowman.

2. *Unworthiness, Inferiority, Shame, Self-Pity.* The soul cannot function effectively without proper self-love. We cannot be a whole person without respecting ourselves as children of God. (Exaggerated self-pride is the opposite side of the coin, but it, too, limits our functioning.)

3. *Worry, Anxiety, Fear, and Unbelief.* These pains indicate that the soul's faith life is in jeopardy, that our trust in God and his ways is faltering.

4. *Despair, Discouragement, Frustration.* Here, too, the soul has been damaged, for hope in God's promises and reliance on his strength and wisdom is a sign that the soul is healthy and growing.

5. *Grief, Sorrow, Sadness.* Whether the pain's source is legitimate (real) or imaginary, a soul needs comfort to survive and thrive once again.

6. *Covetousness, Lust, Greed.* These symptoms signal a misdirected and improperly applied attempt of the soul to be contented, at rest, and satisfied.

7. *Guilt (Legitimate).* Here the soul is being warned of its need to repent and receive the healing that comes with forgiveness.

8. *Doubt.* Indecisiveness warns of unfaithfulness and breeds inertia. The double-minded soul needs the surgery of spiritual circumcision.

9. *Apathy, Indifference.* These pains indicate numbness of the soul's sensory apparatus.

10. *Anger, Depression.* (Depression is anger internalized and gone cold.) These emotions expose those areas where we have not reckoned ourselves dead to our supposed rights.

11. *Bitterness, Resentment.* When these negative emotions are allowed to direct the soul's activities, its "forgiveness" mechanisms are damaged.

Constructive Purposes of Pain

We are able to *choose* a behavior that causes pain, for constructive purposes. Although it is not the thrust of this chapter, we need to recognize this, so I will refer to it briefly. There are at least three avenues we can take that involve pain but yet are profitable in building and maturing the soul.

The Way of Development and Enlargement. "No pain, no gain" is a statement a bodybuilder might make about his gym time. Some individuals submit themselves to vigorous exercises and special diets to develop their physical body. Though their muscles ache, they voluntarily push themselves through difficult, repetitious exercise as they drive themselves to reach their goals.

To develop soul strength, we can suffer the pain of self-denial. As we submit to our Lord, he often asks us to deny ourselves certain activities so we can take up something new for the kingdom. Saying no to long-established habits and many personal desires and preferences brings pain. To conform to a Christian lifestyle, we adopt certain disciplines, some of which cause a certain amount of suffering and inconvenience (see Part Three), but true change is seldom painless.

Hebrews 12:2 says of Jesus, "Who for the joy set before Him endured the cross, despising the shame." He knew there was a joy he could not experience without suffering and chose the way of suffering to attain that joy for himself and all mankind.

Look at the victory he won by being a lamb slain. He refused to be a lion. He could have been. Look at the power he had. Remember how the disciples wanted him to call down fire, and how he refused. Christians, even in their imperfections, are evidence of the lamb slain, rather than the lion loosed.

Moses tried the lion-loosed method, and lost. The second time, he let the Lord be his strength, and the Lord's way is the lamb-slain method, the Passover.

The Way to Unify Christians. I quickly go into action when a single part of my body is hurting. So, too, does physical tragedy bring people together in the world to seek mutual healing.

Pain experienced in the body of Christ—his church—is the quickest way to achieving unity. We will never be completely unified by doctrine, by experience, by programs—but we can be united by pain among the brethren, simply because there is so much of it. Pain is a universal condition of the human body, mind, and spirit. How best to handle our own and others' soul pain will be the topic of the remaining chapters of *Soul Care*.

. . . both God and life will maturity. But they do more than passively will our maturity; they conspire in every possible way, short of breaking down our wills, to make us mature. Life makes us discontented and unhappy in our immaturities. Suppose we could settle down happy and contented in being a half-person, then that would be a tragic situation. But we cannot. Divine discontent is a goal that impels us into higher, fuller life. Life won't let us settle down—to nothingness.

And what kind of Father would God be if He did not disturb us toward maturity? No earthly parent could be content to have a child who refused to grow up. The parents' joy is in development, in growth, in going on toward maturity. God cannot be otherwise and still be God, our Father. So the disturbances we feel in our immaturities are not signs of His anger, but a manifestation of His love. He loves us too much to let us settle down in half-wayness.

DeVern Fromke
Unto Full Stature

14

An Umpire for the Soul

On the popular TV series, "People's Court" Judge Wapner settles differences between people. Watching this program, you will notice that people on both sides of each case are fully convinced that *they* are right and the other party is wrong. Interviewed on their way out of the courtroom, the losers usually express amazement and anger that the judge found them "guilty," or decided against them.

Judge Wapner is really an *umpire* for people who can't agree. Just as we need umpire-judges for legal problems, we need an outside authority to settle disputes and guide our decisions in other areas.

We usually associate the word *umpire* with baseball, our national sport. Here, umpires are trained officials authorized to rule on all the plays made during a game. They decide whether a ball is fair or foul, whether a player is safe or out, whether a pitch is a strike or ball, even when to call a game because of rain.

Other "umpires" have varying levels of authority and are called by different names:

In society, to administer our laws, they are judges.
In football, they are referees.
In the building trade, they are inspectors.
In labor disputes, they are mediators or arbitrators.
In literary fields, they are censors.
In art, they are art critics.
In marriage conflict, they are counselors.

The Need for an Outside Opinion

One of the reasons we need umpires is our limited and often self-serving point of view.

My small grandson Arthur screamed, "It's mine." Then he tried to wrestle the Snickers candy bar away from Richie, his older brother. Richie responded with equal vigor: "It's mine!" Following these shouts, a lot of pushing and shoving culminated in a few well-placed blows and more yelling and crying. Mama Debbie rushed in, separated the antagonists, and then wisely arbitrated the argument.

As the story unfolded, Debbie learned that someone had given Arthur the Snickers. From his limited point of view, he was entitled to that candy. Investigator Debbie discovered that both boys had been given candy bars, but Arthur left his on the floor and the dog ate it. So he attempted to take Richie's. Debbie acted as an umpire, finally returning the Snickers bar to its rightful owner.

Just like three-year-old Arthur, we are often only able to see one side of an issue. Furthermore, our limited point of view is usually prejudiced and/or selfish. Not a single one of us is without bias, since our culture, training, talents, experience, and sinful nature make up our attitudes. Since prejudices keep us from seeing clearly, we may need an objective outsider to help us know what is right, to compensate for our blind spots.

To all this, add the human tendency to superficiality. Most of us are surface people. Unless there is real discipline, we react according to the externals of a situation. We judge by appearances, and live by feelings and impulses. We rarely take the time to look deeply into matters to find truth, the reality that lies behind the obvious.

Identifying the Umpire for the Soul

God, in his tender mercy, has given us an umpire for the soul, an umpire who can judge between right and wrong, between the Holy Spirit and the evil one. This umpire senses approaching evil and cautions us against doing wrong. (He also lets us know when we have already done wrong.) This umpire's presence—even his whistle-blowing—is a continual witness that we are on the right track. His absence is a sign that we are in danger and headed for trouble.

The umpire for the soul is the peace of Christ! Paul spells this out clearly: "And let the peace of Christ rule in your hearts . . ." (Col. 3:15). Another Bible version is more specific: "The peace that Christ gives is to guide you in the decisions you make . . ." (TEV).

What is this peace of God? For hours I struggled to find ways to describe the umpire for the soul. Then I realized what Paul meant when he referred to "the peace of God, which surpasses all comprehension" (Phil. 4:7). If something is beyond my understanding, I will have a very difficult time expressing it in familiar terms. Keeping that inadequacy in mind, I will make an attempt anyway.

Grace and Peace

Readers of the New Testament immediately recognize a common greeting and blessing: "Grace and peace from God the Father to you." Notice that grace is always listed before peace, because there can be no peace without God's grace. But there *can* be grace-consciousness without a sense of peace.

Many people realize that because of God's grace, they are fully accepted in Christ, their sins are forgiven, access to God is a reality, and they are sons and daughters of God.

They do not doubt their relationship with God, but they do not know the peace he offers. They know of the salvation that grace provides, but they do not experience his rest.

Quite obviously, the New Testament writers recognized not only the difference between grace and peace but also their connection. Both come from God and Christ, the sole distributor of these precious blessings.

Peace *with and* of *God*

Even those who know peace *with* God often do not understand the peace *of* God and how to attain it. There is a difference between the two concepts:

> Therefore having been justified by faith, we have peace *with* God through our Lord Jesus Christ (Rom. 5:1, italics mine).
> And the peace *of* God, which surpasses all comprehension, shall guard your hearts and your minds in Christ Jesus (Phil. 4:7, italics mine).

Peace *with* God refers to a relationship, while the peace *of* God refers to the confidence that comes out of understanding and living in the implications of that relationship.

A man can know that God is his Father and Christ his Lord, and still have an aching soul. Only after we understand what it means for God to be Father and Christ to be Lord do we begin to live and appropriate this truth. Then we can begin to experience the peace of God.

Joe is a Christian and never doubts it. His lifestyle and his talk proves this. But Joe is a chronic worrier. His words betray his fears. He is constantly talking about his work, mainly whether or not he will lose his job at NASA. Joe has peace *with* God, not the peace *of* God.

Amy is a Christian, an excellent wife and mother and a respectable church member. But she cannot entrust God with her children's future. Her conversation about her children focuses on some future trouble they might get into. Amy has peace *with* God, but not the peace *of* God.

There is no better area of life for Christians to bear witness to a fearful world than by walking in the peace of God. As people see us in peace, even in terrible circumstances, they will begin to ask what we have and how we got it.

Peace in the Spirit

The Christian's soul is one in which the Holy Spirit lives. When the Spirit in us is undisturbed, our soul is at peace. When we are disturbed, it is because the Holy Spirit is in the words of Scripture—"grieved" or "quenched."

Have you ever sensed inner unrest and not known why? Nothing outward was bothering you, no adverse circumstances or troublesome people, but you were uneasy.

This tells you that the umpire for your soul is sending his warning, to keep you out of trouble or tell you that you are already in a mess.

After a $1,000 loss you can't afford, peace in the Spirit is waking up with this thought: *God, we lost $1,000. We're $1,000 poorer today than we were yesterday*—followed by God's response: "Yes, I know, but *I'm* not worried about how we're going to make up the deficit because I know you can work it out, with my guidance."

Peace in the Spirit is realizing you are so close to God that your loss is his loss. It is knowing he is in the boat with you. He has the same interests and investments you have.

A counselor once listened to an adult's account of his abusive childhood. At the end the counselor asked, "What do you think God was doing while this was going on?"

The abused man-child said, "He was crying." This man had peace in his soul—peace in the Spirit—even though a lot of dreadful things had happened to him. Peace in the Spirit is knowing that God identifies and empathizes this closely with us. Our pain is his pain. Our tears are his tears. Our joy is his joy.

Another way of understanding peace in the Spirit is to look at some of the synonyms and antonyms for peace. Negatively speaking, the peace of God is the *absence* of:

doubt	concern	suspicion
worry	misgiving	horror
fear	apprehension	panic
anxiety	terror	restlessness
anguish	dread	nervousness
uneasiness	care	tension

Positively speaking, the peace of God is the *presence* of:

hope	trust
confidence	expectation
assurance	optimism
security	tranquility

The Peace of Christ's Presence

The peace *of* God is only possible when there is a consciousness of his presence. Christ sustains our peace. Christ knows that he is Lord of all and therefore is at perfect peace. He is not worried or perturbed about anything, not wringing his hands about this world. He knows how it all turns out. He has the peace of God and gives it to us by his presence.

God's peace is the peace a child senses in his mother's arms. It is the peace one has when escorted by a police officer through a rough area of town. It is the peace a traveler has on an unknown journey when he has a reputable guide.

Years ago I was riding by a slum in a Third World country. It was so bad that the government surrounded the area with a high fence to hide it. Sticking above this fence and attached to a tin shack in the middle of the slum, was a large sign in red letters: "If Christ is in the boat, we will not fear the storm." What a testimony! In the middle of these awful circumstances was an individual who knew the peace of God.

The peace of God comes by our consciousness of the presence of the eternal Christ. In his hand lies all power and authority, yet he loves and cares for me and is totally committed in covenant to my care and well-being.

The peace of God comes when this ever-present Christ speaks words of comfort and assures me that all will be well.

> The peace of God is something that I experience,
> not after the storm but in the storm,
> not after the war but during the war,
> not after the sun arrives but in the middle of
> darkness,
> not after the money comes but while I still
> need it,

not after the children are grown and well-married
   but while they are away from home or with their
   friends.

The peace of the world occurs after the fact, after a trouble has been resolved. But the peace of God—the peace
of Christ's presence—is experienced *during* the fact, no
matter how bad it is.

With God's peace you will sing praises at midnight
and know the meaning of Habakkuk 3:17–18:

Though the fig tree should not blossom,
And there be no fruit on the vines,
Though the yield of the olive should fail,
And the fields produce no food,
Though the flock should be cut off from the fold,
And there be no cattle in the stalls,
Yet will I exult in the LORD,
I will rejoice in the God of my salvation.

Such peace is much more than the absence of fear and
worry. It reflects an awareness of the indwelling power
of him who loves and cares for us. The peace of Christ's
presence comes when we, by deliberate choice, place
everything in our Lord's hands and leave it there. We are
thereby acknowledging that he is Lord of all and trusting him to work out any difficulty or problem we may
have.

Letting the Soul's Umpire Rule

I let God's umpire rule in my soul when his peace is
the determining factor in my life. I willingly bow to this
authority's presence and will and am guided by the
"peace umpire" rather than by *my* emotions, reasonings, desires. When I lose the peace of God, I stop everything until I regain it.

Have you ever been having a wonderful day when suddenly a heaviness creeps over you for some unknown reason? Have you tried to figure out what happened? Many times, I can assure you, it was your soul's umpire warning you that something needed attention.

How does this work? The umpire for your soul can withdraw the peace of God, allowing worry, or one of its cousins, to enter your inner man. The umpire first signals to get your attention and then makes his ruling.

Occasionally, in conversation with another brother, I will criticize someone else. I lose immediately my sense of inner peace. Then I know God has blown his official whistle, requiring me to get back in the boundaries of play and stick to the rules, which include, "Do not judge your brother." Peace returns when I stop the critical remarks and make whatever restitution is necessary.

Peace is also lost when the evil one attacks, disturbing my soul's tranquillity with deception. When this happens, I must stop to let God speak his peace in and to me and thus restore my spiritual equilibrium.

A Testimony

No other person I know has learned how to allow the peace of God to umpire in heart and soul any better than my wife, Johnnie. The following is part of the testimony she gave in one of our Sunday-morning services:

> I have found that just as sure as I'm going to share a particular truth, I will have an opportunity to prove it. This weekend there was a ladies' retreat at Satellite Beach, and they had asked me to speak on "Walking in Peace."
>
> But guess what happened yesterday morning. Just before 6 A.M., I got up to pray and go over my notes. I found I'd picked up the wrong notebook. There were no notes along the line that I was going to be sharing. I

thought, What am I going to do? I'd prepared for this retreat, and now all my notes are gone.

As I began getting apprehensive, I did what I found always works. I sought God and said, "Now, Lord, you know that I think I don't have anything that will help these ladies, but I'm convinced that you do."

Let me just explain to you what process goes on for me when I would normally be apprehensive. I talk the situation over with the Lord until I'm settled in my heart, until he gives me reassurance, until I am at peace.

Now I do not think it correct to assume that we will never have disturbances come into our life. That's not reality, for the enemy can always shoot a dart at us to disturb our peace. What I've found is that if I will not take another step—if I will deal with that issue, talk it out, pray it through, let the Lord show me anything I have to do to settle that issue before I go on—that's the way he has provided for me to walk in peace.

When Philippians 4:6 says that we're to be anxious about nothing, nothing is what it means. And when it says we're to pray about everything, everything is what it means. Not a general "Lord, give me peace," but a specific request about that matter.

There are other times when a lot of issues have come together and I have delayed in taking care of them properly. When many circumstances are involved, I have to sit down, write them out, one point at a time, being specific in giving each one to the Lord, talking them through with him. I have found that it's very helpful before I leave an issue to ask the Lord to tell me what he's going to do about a situation.

That's like yesterday at the ladies' retreat. I said, "Lord, now I'm going to trust you. Would you reassure me? I'm just a child, so I need to hear. Would you let me hear you say that you're going to be with me? I'll be all right if I know you are." And he very patiently, lovingly, and faithfully reassured me.

At other times and with different issues, the only way that I get peace from God is by cooperating with him, doing the things he leads me to do to resolve those issues. Sometimes there are situations he takes care of by himself, but there are many times that I must take action and be a part of my peace being re-established. I may have to write a letter, make a phone call. Sometimes it's an apology; sometimes it's just to communicate love to somebody.

There's no limit to the different actions it might involve. But I'm convinced that God provided his peace not only through Christ and his shed blood, but through his Spirit's coming to live in us. This walk of peace involves both my relationship with God and my relationship with other people. If there is something standing between you and me, I've got to be willing to be part of working this thing out in order for me to have peace in my heart again. "Pursue peace with all men, and the sanctification without which no one will see the Lord" (Heb. 12:14).

Sometimes it's peace with myself that I need. Whatever the issue, peace is too precious to just go on down the road and lay it aside, saying, "I'll get back to that later." Because when you are not at peace in your soul, it affects the way you act, the way you feel, the way you respond.

This peace is our most precious possession. It's valuable because it's God's way of telling us that things are all right. When peace is absent, we will not experience it again until we settle the disturbing issue. Whatever you're apprehensive about, let him reassure you. One foundational truth helps me the most. It is remembering *who* came in when I invited Christ into my life. Colossians 2:9 says that God poured himself into the man Christ Jesus, and he's the one I invited in. Almighty God lives inside of me, and he's big enough and smart enough and powerful enough to take care of any situation or relationship that could cause me anxiety—if I trust him and allow him to take charge.

As soon as a tough situation develops, that's the time to work through it. Don't expect it to go away. Go to God and allow him to show you how to handle it. Then be willing to trust him and take whatever action is necessary to bring back the peace of God.

In the Middle Ages
not even the greatest saints
attempted the depths of the inward journey
without the help of a spiritual director.
Today the concept is hardly understood,
let alone practiced,
except in the Catholic monastic system.
That is a tragedy,
for the idea of the spiritual director
is highly applicable
to the contemporary scene.
It is a beautiful expression
of divine guidance
through the help
of our brothers and sisters.

Richard Foster
Celebration of Discipline

15

The Spiritual Director

Billie,
Do you know anyone who could do a one-on-one with
me? I need someone to help me stick with my walk with
the Lord. You may call me at home. Thanks.

Sheri

A young mother in our church placed this note on my
secretary's desk. Sheri's appeal is for what has been
called in church history a *spiritual director.* Sheri has
recognized a basic truth about soul care and the spiritual
life—there are some things we cannot do alone.

The early settlers of the West employed guides to take
them on the new and perilous journey across our conti-
nent. These experienced travelers knew the safest and
easiest way, where to find water, when to use the moun-
tain passes, how to avoid Indian ambushes. The guides
had already made the journey successfully many times
and now could direct others.

The same idea can be applied to the spiritual realm. Both at the beginning of our walk as Christians and all along the way, we need other people to help keep us on course—to fellowship with us, minister to and love us, and ease our trip. At various times in life we will need one or more spiritual directors.

You might be saying, "I have the Holy Spirit to guide me. Isn't that enough?" Yes, you do have the Helper, the Comforter, but you also need some human support, if only to help you recognize the Spirit's guidance. Though the Holy Spirit guides us into all truth, as Jesus promised (John 16:13), it is in God's plan that he works much of our guidance through other people. This is why the body of Christ—the church—is continually strengthened by what is given through each member.

Any Christian who has been on the Christian walk for any length of time knows there are times when we cannot seem to find God, when we mistake light for darkness and darkness for light. It is then that we become confused and lose our way, then that we need another to help us.

This is like the little boy who was afraid and whose mother sought to comfort him by her assurance that "God is with you." The little boy replied, "I know that, Mommy, but I need to see a real body—skin and bones and muscles." There are times when we all need to "see a real body."

The term *spiritual director* is very rare in the religious culture and tradition of most of us. Not only is the term practically unknown, but the function is rarely practiced. The result is that many Christians have never left spiritual infancy. They had no guide for the journey.

Writing on this matter, Kenneth Leech says in *Soul Friend*, "The gulf between academic theology and the exercise of pastoral care and spiritual guidance has been disastrous for all concerned." We could use many other terms to describe the function of the spiritual director, including tour guide, spiritual companion, soul friend, shepherd, discipler. What is important is not the title but the *function*.

Modern Shepherds

Some churches have a pastor who is truly a spiritual director to the congregation. Those members are very fortunate but in the minority, for most "pastors" are no longer *pastors*. They are *preachers*, and that is what we should call them. Typical seminary training is irrelevant to providing soul care since it ignores the fine points of pastoral leadership and shepherding. Many Christian ministers do not know how to function this way. Basically, most of them preach on Sunday and provide emergency-room care for the critically injured and dysfunctional people during the week. In addition, depending on the denomination, they run the "organization" in varying degrees.

In most churches it is impossible for the minister to shepherd the flock. Why? Because there are too many people and too much is expected of the spiritual leader. In such a case, he or she needs to be training lay pastors.

Referring to the Good Shepherd (*see* John 10:1–18), Jesus stated the most basic, necessary truth about pastoring—the shepherd knows his sheep, and his sheep know him (v. 14). Mutual "knowing" is the basis of all discipleship. Shepherding is a *personal* relationship developed through genuine communication and sharing, as well as guidance given and received.

It is very beneficial for new Christians to have a competent shepherd directing them through the growth stages of Christian faith. As pastor of a large church, I try to locate a lay pastor for every new Christian, but my big problem is having adequate and willing people to do this. Unfortunately, modern church life is often not conducive to maturing our people—and children never do a good job taking care of babies! One of my purposes in writing this book is to correct this condition.

Margo, a friend's wife, is one of the most able spiritual directors I know. She says she became this way because a loving woman in Miami once took her under her wing and became her spiritual guide and mentor. This is part of Margo's testimony:

> Before becoming a pastor, my husband was an insurance salesman in southwest Miami. One day, while visiting Liz Hand, he saw a Thompson Chain Reference Bible on her coffee table. He mentioned that I might be interested in seeing such a study Bible. Liz offered to visit me and bring along this Bible.
>
> This is how I met my spiritual "mother in the faith." I was already born again and had been studying the Bible each week to help me teach Sunday school. But during her regular visits, I began to see that Liz was a woman who not only knew God's Word but knew God. This began our relationship, which today is called "discipling."
>
> The monthly visits continued for more than two years. Liz always brought me Bible-study books and listened to my problems in trying to care for four children. Childless, her counsel always came from God's Word. Looking back, I can see God designing this relationship so that I could not only know His Word better, but I could truly know *Him.* He used Liz as "bait," so I would press on to know Him at least as well as she did.
>
> When we moved away from Miami, Liz continued to disciple me by writing. She would send letters with Scripture verses for different situations that I was living through, or mail me books to read. Thirty years later, she still does these things for me.

Because God used Liz Hand, my spiritual mother, to nourish me as she did, I have used her as a model over the years to nourish other women.

Characteristics of a Spiritual Director

Examining the qualifications of a spiritual director will help you if you are looking for one or trying to become one yourself. These are not listed in order of importance.

Maturity

"Maturity" is not perfection. Rather, it means that someone is farther down the Christian road than you are. Christian maturity is not measured by *time* on the road, however. (There are many who have been Christians for twenty years but have never grown.) A mature Christian has learned to cope successfully with a variety of situations and events. He or she has learned through mistakes and is a seasoned traveler, ready to share with someone else.

Transparency

Beware of mentors who are not open and honest about feelings! Transparent people will share with you their own past and present—their failures and success, weakness and strengths, fears and joys. An effective guide will be aboveboard in what he or she says, and you will be encouraged by this display of honesty.

Exemplification

Spiritual directors must guide by example first and instruction second, carefully living out the truths they preach. In Acts 1:1, Luke refers to his record of Christ's life as "The first account I composed [The Gospel of Luke], Theophilus, about all that Jesus began to *do* and

teach." Note the order of the two words I have itali-
cized.

Unconditional Love

A spiritual director will love you regardless of your
performance or what you confess. Those providing soul
care for others must be unflappable! Because they are
aware of their own sin and what they might be capable
of doing in the future, they are never surprised at the
behavior of another person. Even when you are moody,
angry over a recent failure, or generally unreceptive to
their guidance on a given day, they will receive you as
you are. This is like the relentless love a good mother
has for a child. It takes maturity to develop, which
explains why there are so many dropout parents in both
the spiritual and physical realms of life.

Patience

Wise shepherds never try to rush the growth process.
They understand that people come from many different
backgrounds: pagan or religious, educated or un-
schooled, socially skilled or provincial. We could go on
and on, but it is simpler to say that because no person is
exactly like another, each must be dealt with as an individual. (Every parent with more than one child can identify with this truth.) While all Christians are headed in
the same direction, we arrive there by different paths. A
spiritual director must recognize this and be patient—
careful not to set arbitrary standards for measuring
growth.

Personally, I make an agreement with those I lead
that goes something like this: I will never ask you to do
anything that you do not believe Christ wants you to do
now. When I suggest things to do, you must ask the

Holy Spirit if it is right for you. Then you can act out of faith that he is walking with you.

Once a man I was discipling asked me if he should quit smoking. I replied, "I don't have the answer for that one. Why not ask the Lord?" I try to nudge people into a living relationship with Christ because he will always be around; I will not. He will always be right; I will not. New Christians need to learn to depend on him, not on their spiritual mentor.

This man did ask the Lord. The Lord told him he did not at that moment have to stop smoking. Does that seem strange to you? If it does, you need to know God's ways a little better. It means you have a preconceived idea of what Christ will tell each person.

A spiritual director's job is not to give a list of dos and don'ts but to assist a person into a continuous relationship with the indwelling Christ. This takes a lot of patience, because God works in his own special way and time for every individual.

Availability

A good tour guide for your soul is available when needed, which usually means when you're in trouble. This describes the availability of a mother to a child, and it is one of the reasons a person should not try to disciple many people at the same time.

Submission

One sign of maturity is realizing that we never get to the place where we don't need others. Spiritual adults know they have besetting sins, possibly deceptions, blind spots, undeveloped areas. They understand the place of "body life," that the Lord feeds individuals through other members of the body of Christ, the church. Therefore, a spiritual guide must be open to

input from others if he or she is truly submitted to
God's authority.

A popular Christian speaker and author who fell into
sin in the 1980s testified, "I had no one I was close to,
no one I could share my heart with." This man was
attempting to guide others through his books, sermons,
and leadership position. Yet he had no guide himself—
and so he got lost. Praise God, he is now being restored
and testifies that he has surrounded himself with people
to guide him.

Paul of Hungary in his *Summa Magistri Pauli* (1120)
gave this description of a spiritual director:

> *Let him be inclined to correct kindly and to bear the*
> *weight himself. He must be gentle and affectionate,*
> *merciful to the faults of others. He shall act with dis-*
> *cernment in different cases. Let him aid his penitent*
> *with prayer, alms, and other good works. He is to help*
> *him by calming his fear, consoling him, giving him*
> *back hope, and, if need be, by reproving him. Let him*
> *show compassion in his words and teach by his deeds.*
> *Let him take part in the sorrow, if he wishes to share in*
> *the joy. He must inculcate perseverance.*
>
> Kenneth Leech in *Soul Friend*
> Harper & Row, 1988

Functions of a Spiritual Director

Developing Christ-Consciousness

First and foremost, a spiritual director keeps one
pointed toward Christ, reminding the disciple of what
Christ did, is still doing, and will do in the future. An
ever-increasing awareness of Christ's presence and love
is the greatest source of strength for a Christian who is
still learning that only the Lord offers the promise of
eternal glory.

Interpreting Life's Events and Experiences

One aspect of immaturity is the inability to interpret properly what is going on and why. As a growing Christian shares the experiences of daily life, the spiritual mentor can often put these events into proper perspective. Often, for example, what individuals regard as evidence of God's forsaking them was actually proof of his love, drawing them closer, instructing, and refining their faith. It is easier to survive misfortune if we can recognize a good reason why it happened.

Hearing Confession/Granting God's Forgiveness

There is great therapeutic value in confessing one's sins to another, just as there is healing in hearing from a brother or sister in Christ that God has forgiven us: "Therefore, confess your sins to one another, and pray for one another, so that you may be healed. The effective prayer of a righteous man can accomplish much" (James 5:16). Shepherding also involves helping babes-in-Christ to seek God's forgiveness (and that of an injured party) *directly*.

Recognizing Danger

A mature Christian has learned the signs of approaching trouble and so can help beginners recognize what they could never see by themselves. For example, a spiritual shepherd might need to warn of the potential danger in these situations:

Keeping the wrong company
Neglecting one's spouse
Not properly discipling or disciplining children
Living above one's income
Discipling someone of the opposite sex

Encouraging

We all need the spiritual food of consistent encouragement if we are to grow: "But encourage one another day after day, as long as it is still called 'Today,' lest any one of you be hardened by the deceitfulness of sin" (Heb. 3:13). Discouragement is a basic tool of the enemy. Spiritual directors know how to encourage because they have been encouraged in the past and wish to share this comfort with others, as Paul reminded us all: "Blessed be the God and Father of our Lord Jesus Christ, the Father of mercies and God of all comfort; who comforts us in all our affliction so that we may be able to comfort those who are in any affliction with the comfort with which we ourselves are comforted by God" (2 Cor. 1:3–4).

Instructing/Facilitating Change

Instruct. We all need ongoing instruction in the basic disciplines of Christian life—how to read the Bible, how to pray effectively, how to forgive, and how best to relate to others. A spiritual director can add to our knowledge about these processes and assist us in putting them into regular practice.

Facilitate. Spiritual directors do not need to have a specific answer for everything, but they must be knowledgeable and willing to help their charges find their own answers.

Providing Friendship

A true companion-in-Christ is, above all, a friend. Being a spiritual director is more than taking on one more church-connected assignment. It is a relationship. Your Christian mentor is preferably someone to whom you are already related in a small-group setting (see chapter 11). If he or she is a person with whom you come into contact during the general flow of your spiritual life, it will save time and seem more natural for both of you. The more time we spend with another person, the easier it becomes to communicate in depth. Remember, too, that a soul friend sticks closer than a brother!

Epilogue

Do we really believe the implied answers to the two questions Jesus asked: *What shall it profit a man if he gains the whole world and damages his own soul?* and *What shall a man give in exchange for his soul?* If we are sure that our souls are our most important possession, we will give them proper care. When we believe something is precious, we will be very diligent about preserving it. We all act according to what we think is true, and, to a great extent, our behavior is based on what we consider is valuable.

But how does one recognize God's truth? Is it the Baptists' truth? (If so, *which* Baptists?) The Methodists' truth? The truths of Roman Catholicism? Which "version" of God's truth are you to follow?

The answer is that you are only obligated to keep the truth that God gives to *you*, to live according to the light that God has placed before you. Someone else's understanding of God's truth is not necessarily accurate or complete for your circumstances. We will never have the peace of God until we quit trying to get other people to live up to our ideas of truth or trying to live up to the "truths" that God has given to another. This sort of uncertainty brings more frustration, anger, and hypocrisy that we can ever imagine—and it is not good for the soul!

How Can I Know?

So, how *can* you know what comes from God? The basic way is to know God well enough to identify his voice. But there are a few additional suggestions that may help.

Stop listening to so many tapes, reading so many books, attending so many meetings and retreats— and instead use that time to get to know God (see chapter 10 for some guidelines). Of course, having a close, mature "spiritual director" whom you can check with may be helpful, so long as you are always responsive to the Holy Spirit's direct leading.

Whenever you have been to church or Sunday-school or in a small-group setting where you have heard someone say that you *ought* to do such-and-such (remember, you can "prove" almost anything logically if you select the appropriate Bible passage), get alone with the Lord and ask him if this is really right for you.

Finally, never forget that we are all in different stages in our Christian growth, and God does not ask everyone to do the same thing in like situations. Obey God's directives for your particular circumstances until doing so becomes a natural part of your life. Then you will see yourself being changed.

Consistency and endurance over the long haul furnish the secret to success in both the worldly and spiritual realms. Average people who persevere are more likely to reach a goal than any superman who does not. Jesus says, "By your perseverance you will win your souls" (Luke 21:19 NAS).

One of the keys to change, growth, health, and soul care is perseverance. It is implied in every biblical success formula, including these:

> [Paul says:] Therefore having been justified by faith, we have peace with God through our Lord Jesus Christ, through whom also we have obtained our introduction by faith into this grace in which we stand; and we exult in hope of the glory of God. And not only this, but we also exult in our tribulations, knowing that tribulation brings about *perseverance*; and *perseverance*, proven character; and proven character, hope (Rom. 5:1–4, italics mine).

> [Peter says:] Now for this very reason also, applying all diligence, in your faith supply moral excellence, and in your moral excellence, knowledge; and in your knowledge, self-control, and in your self-control, *perseverance*, and in your *perseverance*, godliness; and in your godliness, brotherly kindness, and in your brotherly kindness, love. For if these qualities are yours and are increasing, they render you neither useless nor unfruitful in the true knowledge of our Lord Jesus Christ (2 Peter 1:5–8, italics mine).

> [James says:] Consider it all joy, my brethren, when you encounter various trials; knowing that the testing of your faith produces endurance [*perseverance*]. And let endurance have its perfect result, that you may be perfect and complete, lacking in nothing (James 1:2–4, italics mine).

> [The writer of Hebrews says:] For you have need of endurance, so that when you have done the will of God, you may receive what was promised. . . . But we are not of those who shrink back to destruction, but of those who have faith to the preserving of the soul" (Heb. 10:36, 38).

Perseverance usually appears in the King James Version as "patience" and in other versions as "endurance." It is made up of two Greek words: *hupo* ("under") and *meno* ("remain together," meaning "remain under existing pressure").

Perseverance is keeping on keeping on—until what you are doing becomes fully integrated into your lifestyle. By perseverance we will be victorious. Our souls will be discipled so that our potential is fully developed for the glory of God and our own well-being.

One of my favorite jokes is about a man lying in a hospital bed and just coming back into a conscious state after a serious bout of food poisoning. He says to the nurse, "The last thing I remember was saying I can eat anything the natives can."

People traveling abroad are constantly warned as "strangers" to abstain from the local water and food. In some places, we are even told not to clean our teeth in the water, lest our bodies be contaminated.

As a Christian with a new life, you need to be very careful about contaminating your soul. Peter says, "Beloved, I urge you as aliens and strangers to abstain from fleshly lusts, which wage war against the soul" (1 Peter 2:11).

> *abstain*—to hold one's self from (the antonym is to pursue)
> *fleshly*—human nature without God
> *lusts*—conscious impulses towards an object or experience that promises enjoyment or satisfaction on its attainment (longing or craving)
> *war*—attack on the soul to keep it from its purpose.
> *aliens*—a common Greek word of the time, describing someone living temporarily in a country not his own

Soul care demands that you recognize the dangers inherent in fleshly lusts that deceive the mind, distort the emotions, and weaken or captivate the will.

Everyone has a besetting sin, an Achilles' heel of extreme vulnerability. Do you know what yours is?

Some of the more common obsessions are clearly seen by the numbers of people who have succumbed to them: sexual lust, chemical dependency, materialism. Whatever yours is, recognize its existence and stay away from anything that feeds it and strengthens its hold upon you.

If your besetting sin happens to be sexual lust, refuse to watch the TV programs that would exploit your weakness and avoid the books and magazines that would entice you. Stay away from the places where pornography is promoted and from the people who are given over to it. The battle to take care of our souls in a worldly atmosphere is tough enough without needless exposure to those specific things that are going to make it more difficult.

> *Therefore putting aside all filthiness and all that remains of wickedness, in humility receive the word implanted, which is able to save your souls. But prove yourselves doers of the word, and not merely hearers who delude themselves* (James 1:21–22).

Those two sentences sum up all you really need to know about SOUL CARE.

Appendix
The Changed Life
A Sermon by Henry Drummond

I'm including Henry Drummond's sermon on *The Changed Life,* because it gives an answer to the Christian's deep desire for holiness and fulfillment.

Drummond's basic premise is based on teachings given to us in the New Testament; not just a proof text or two, but on the entire thrust of the New Testament. This is the way Jesus lived and the way the early disciples became what they were.

The simplicity of the message is striking. Anybody can live like this regardless of education, background, wealth, or any of the other factors. The one requirement is desire.

His thesis is supported by past saints whose lives and messages have lived on testifying of their ingenuous discovery. Jeanne Guyon recorded her discovery in *Experiencing the Depths of Jesus Christ.* Others preserved Brother Lawrence's experiences along this same path in *Practicing the Presence. The Game with Minutes* is Frank Laubach's classic record of this simple secret. These three, along with Henry Drummond, say the same thing in a different way.

This message exalts Jesus and makes him the sole cause of the effect of holiness. Given seventy-five years ago, I have edited it for easier reading and comprehension.

Part One—Various Methods

"I want to be good—pure." This theme, in the heart of mankind, is as old as man himself. Everyone at some time or other makes this same confession in his inner being. We're all searching for a way to satisfy this longing.

Is this goodness and purity possible? Yes. Under the right conditions it is as natural for character to become perfected as it is for a seed to turn into a beautiful flower. Man was created to develop—to grow, not stop. We see this in Romans 8:29, "For whom he foreknew, he also predestined to become conformed to the image of his Son."

247

Inadequate Ways of Changing Life

Let's begin by naming, and in part discarding, some methods for producing superior lives. These methods are far from wrong; in their place they may even be essential. I disregard them only because they do not turn out the most perfect possible work.

Self-sufficient method. The first imperfect method is to rely on determination. There is no deliverance in will-power and sincerity. Struggle, effort, even agony, have their place in Christianity; but this is not where they come in.

A sailing ship suddenly stopped in the middle of the Atlantic Ocean. Something was wrong with the engines. There were five hundred able-bodied men on board the ship. If they had gathered together and pushed against the masts could they have pushed it on?

When one attempts to sanctify/purify himself by effort, he is trying to make his boat go by pushing against the mast. He is like a drowning man trying to lift himself out of the water by pulling on the hair of his own head. Christ held up this method almost to ridicule when he said, "Which of you by taking thought can add a cubit to his stature?" The one redeeming feature of the self-sufficient method is that those who try it find out almost at once that it will not achieve the goal.

Self-eliminate evil method. You may say, "I'm not so naive. That is not my method. A wild struggle in the dark is misguided. I work on a principle. My plan is not to waste power on random effort, but to concentrate on a single sin. By taking one sin at a time and crucifying it steadily, I hope in the end to eliminate all."

There are at least four objections to this method:

1. Life is too short; the name of sin is Legion.
2. To deal with an individual sin is to leave the rest of the nature untouched for the time being.
3. A single combat with a special sin does not affect the root and source of the disease. If only one of the channels of sin is obstructed, we will have a sin overflow in some other part of our character. Partial transformation is almost always accompanied by moral leakage, because the pent-up energies accumulate to the bursting-point. Then the last state of the soul may be worse than the first.
4. Christianity is not negative—stopping this sin and stopping that sin. The perfect character can never be produced with a pruning knife.

Copy method. Some people decide not to attempt stopping sins one by one. They choose an opposite technique. "I'll copy the virtues one by one." The difficulty with the copy method is that it is apt to be mechanical. One can always tell a print from an original painting, an artificial flower from a real flower. To copy virtues one by one has somewhat the same effect as eradicating the vices one by one; the temporary result is an overbalanced and phony character.

Sometimes we see Christians overfed on one side of their nature, but dismally thin and starved-looking on the other. Copying humility and adding it on to an otherwise worldly life results in a grotesque character.

For example, a rabid teetotaler may be a poor specimen of Christianity, excelling in a single virtue, and quite oblivious that his soapbox is making him worse, not better.

Character is a unit. All the virtues must advance together to make the perfect whole man. This method of sanctification, nevertheless, is in the right direction. Its failure is in implementation.

Journal/diary method. A fourth method is a variation of those already named. A journal is kept with columns for the days of the week, and a list of desirable character traits with spaces against each for check marks. Strict rules, living by code, provide a private judgment bar for the individual. Probably thousands could tell how they drew up rules to shape their lives. This method is not inappropriate, but has poor success. It fails generally for very matter-of-fact reasons; most likely, because one day we forget the rules.

The self-sufficient method, the self-elimination method, the copy method, and the journal/diary method are perfectly human, perfectly natural, perfectly ignorant, and as they stand, perfectly inadequate. I am not arguing that they must be abandoned. Their harm is that they distract attention from the method that really works. They produce a fair result at the expense of the perfect one. What is the perfect method?

Part Two—The Formula of Sanctification

A formula for sanctification? Is this mighty change, this process, as definite as the production of so many volts of electricity? Absolutely!

Shall a mechanical experiment succeed infallibly, and the one vital experiment of humanity remain a chance? Do we grow corn by method, and character by impulse, or hit-and-miss? If we cannot express the law of these forces in simple words, then Christianity is not the world's religion, but the world's great dilemma. Where do we look for such a formula? Among the textbooks.

If we turn to the textbooks of Christianity, we find a formula for solving this problem as clear and precise as any in the mechanical sciences. Following this simple rule produces a perfect character as surely as any harvest guaranteed by the laws of nature.

In Scripture, the finest expression of this rule is in Paul's second letter to the Corinthians. He wrote to Christians seeking the higher life while living in a city known for depravity and licentiousness.

But we all, with unveiled face beholding as in a mirror the glory of the Lord, are being transformed into the same image from glory to glory, just as from the Lord the Spirit (2 Cor. 3:18).

Changed Not Change

"We are being transformed." We are changed; we do not change ourselves. No man changes himself. Throughout the New Testament wherever these moral and spiritual transformations are described, the verbs are in the passive voice. Passive means not active, but acted upon, affected by an outside force. Being passive, however, does not deny all human effort or ignore basic law.

This implication for the spiritual man here is what is claimed for the physical man. In the physical realm the verbs describing the processes of growth are in the passive tense. Growth is not voluntary; it takes place, it happens, it is formed on matter.

So it is in the spiritual.

Scripture tells us, You must be born again. We cannot give birth to ourselves. Do not be conformed to this world, but be transformed (Rom. 8:29). We are subject to a transforming influence. We do not transform ourselves. Just as something outside the thermometer produces a change in the thermometer, something outside the soul of man produces a moral change in him. We understand that he must be a participant in the process, but know that neither his aptitude nor his will can produce it.

The change we are striving after is not produced by more striving. It is formed in us by the molding of hands beyond our own. As the branch ascends, and the bud bursts, and the fruit reddens under the cooperation of influences from the outside air; so man rises to the higher stature under invisible pressures from without.

The First Law of Change

The radical defect of all our former methods of sanctification was the attempt to generate from within that which can be formed in us only from without.

According to the first law of motion everything continues in its state of rest, or of uniform motion in a straight line, until it is compelled by impressed forces to change that state.

This is also a first law of Christianity. Everyone's character remains as it is, or continues in the direction in which it is going, until it is compelled by impressed forces to change that state. Our failure has been the failure to put ourselves in the path of the impressed forces.

There is clay, and there is a potter; we have tried to get the clay to mold the clay.

The formula is "By reflecting as a mirror the glory of the Lord we are changed."

What is the "glory" of the Lord, and how can mortal man reflect it? How can this "reflecting the glory of the Lord" act as an "impressed force" in molding us to a nobler form?

The word *glory*—the word which has to bear the weight of holding those "impressed forces"—is a stranger in current speech; and our first duty is to seek out its equivalent in working English.

It suggests at first a radiance of some kind, something dazzling or glittering, some halo such as the old masters painted round the heads of their portraits of the Christ. But that is paint, mere matter, the visible symbol of some unseen thing. What is that unseen thing? Of all unseen things, it is the most radiant, the most beautiful, the most divine. On earth, in heaven, there is nothing so great, so glorious, as this.

Glory has many meanings; in ethics it only has one. Glory is character. Nothing less, and it can be nothing more. The earth is "full of glory of the Lord," because it is full of his character. The "beauty of the Lord" is character. "The radiance of his glory" is character. "The glory of the only begotten" is character, the character which is "fullness of grace and truth."

When God told his people his name, he simply gave them his character, which was himself: "And the Lord proclaimed the Name of the Lord . . . the Lord, the Lord God, merciful and gracious, long-suffering and abundant in goodness and truth."

Glory then is not something intangible, or ghostly, or transcendental. If it were, then how could Paul ask men to reflect it? Stripped of its physical wrapping it is beauty, moral and spiritual beauty, beauty infinitely real, infinitely exalted, yet infinitely near and infinitely communicable.

With this explanation, read over this paraphrase: A mirror does not create images; it only reflects. We are like a mirror. As we focus on Christ, the reflection of his character transforms us into his image. It is a process—from character to character—from a poor character to a better one, from a better one to one a little better still, from that to one still more complete, until by slow degrees the perfect image is attained.

The solution of the problem of sanctification is compressed into a sentence: Reflect the character of Christ and you will become like Christ.

We Are Mirrors—Law A

All men are mirrors. We absorb impressions and reflect them. In the home a child takes on the mannerisms of a parent and reflects them to his world. The child's teacher says, "Your son reminds me of you. His gestures, the tone of his voice, word choices, and his walk are a mirror image of you."

When we meet a stranger we see a reflection of his whole background. His conversation reflects the books he has read, his home, his friends, and all those events that have influenced him and made him the man he is. These are all registered in him by a pen which lets nothing escape, and whose writing can never be blotted out.

Whether we like it or not, we live in see-through houses. The mind, the memory, the soul, is simply a vast chamber paneled with glass. This miraculous arrangement and endowment gives us the capacity to "reflect the character of the Lord."

But this is not all. If all these varied reflections from our so-called private life are evident to those we meet, think how much more complete the record is in the soul itself. The influences we meet are not simply held for a moment on the polished surface and thrown off again into space. Each is retained where it first fell, and stored up in the soul for ever.

We Are Assimilating Mirrors—Law B

This law of assimilation is the second, and by far the most impressive, truth underlying the formula of sanctification. Men are not only mirrors, mere reflectors of the fleeting things they see, but also transfer into their own innermost being, and hold in permanent preservation the things they reflect.

No one knows how the soul holds these things. No one knows how the miracle is done. No phenomenon in nature, no process in chemistry, no chapter in magic can help us begin to understand this amazing operation. Think of it. The past is not only *focused* in a man's soul, it also *is* there. How could it be reflected if it were not there?

All the things that he has ever seen, known, felt, or believed of the surrounding world are now within him, have become part of him. In part, they are him. He has been changed into their image. He may deny it, resent it; but they are there. They do not adhere to him, they are transfused through him. He cannot alter or rub them out. They are not in his memory, they are in him. His soul is as they have filled it, made it, left it.

These things, these books, these events, these influences are his makers. In their hands are life and death, beauty and deformity. When once the image or likeness of any of these is adequately presented to the soul, no power on earth can hinder two things happening. One, it is absorbed into the soul. And two, the character forever reflects it again.

On these astounding yet perfectly obvious psychological facts, Paul bases his doctrine of sanctification. He sees that character is a thing built up by slow degrees, it is an hourly changing for better or for worse, according to the images which flit across it. How do these ideas apply to the central problem of reflecting the glory of Christ and being changed into his image?

Part Three—*The Alchemy of Influence*

No man can meet another on the street without making some impression on him. We say we exchange words when we meet; what we exchange is souls. When association is close and frequent, so complete is this exchange that recognizable bits of the one soul begin to show in the other's nature; and the second is conscious of a similar and growing debt to the first.

We witness this mysterious process of the drawing together of two souls. We've watched an elderly couple come down life's pilgrimage hand in hand with such gentle trust and joy in one another that their faces wore the same look. These were not two souls; they are a composite soul. It did not matter to which of the two you spoke, you could have said the same words to either. It didn't matter which replied, each would have said the same. Half a century's reflecting had altered them: they were changed into the same image.

The Law of Influence

The law of influence is that we become like those we habitually admire. Through all the range of literature, history, and biography this law dominates. All men are mosaics of other men. There was a quality of David about Jonathan and a quality of Jonathan about David.

The family, the cradle of mankind, has no meaning apart from this. Society itself is nothing but a rallying-point for these omnipotent forces to do their work. The vast pyramid of humanity is built on the doctrine of influence.

Paul made the supreme application of the law of influence. It was a tremendous inference to make, but he never hesitated. He himself was a changed man: he knew exactly what had done it; it was Christ. They met on the Damascus road, and from that hour his life was absorbed in Christ. Paul's words, deeds, career, and creed were forever altered. The "impressed forces" did their vital work. Paul became like him whom he habitually loved.

So we all, he writes, reflecting as a mirror the glory of Christ are changed into the same image.

Nothing could be more simple, more intelligible, more natural, more supernatural. It is an analogy from an everyday fact. Since we are what we are by the impacts of those who surround us, those who surround themselves with the highest will be changed into the high-est. There are some men and women in whose company we are always at our best. While with them we cannot think mean thoughts or speak ungenerous words. Their mere presence is elevation, purifi-cation, sanctity. All the best notes in our nature are drawn out by their conversation, and we find a music in our souls that was never there before.

Imagine their influence prolonged through a month, a year, a life-time, and what would we become? Here, even in ordinary life, are sanctifiers of souls talking our language, walking our streets, and working side by side. Here, breathing through common clay, is a godly influence. If living with godly men can exalt and purify our nature, the influence of living with Christ is unlimited. To live with Socrates—with unveiled face—must have made one wise. Francis of Assisi must have made one gentle; Savonarola, strong. But to have lived with Christ? To have lived with Christ must have made one like Christ; that is to say, a Christian.

As a matter of fact, to live with Christ did produce this effect, in the case of Paul. And during Christ's lifetime the experiment was tried in an even more startling form. A few raw, unspiritual, unin-spiring men, were admitted to the inner circle of his friendship. The change began at once. Day by day we can almost see the first disci-ples grow.

First the faintest possible sketch of his character appears in them, and occasionally, very occasionally, they do a thing, or say a thing that they could not have done or said had they not been living there.

Slowly the spell of his life deepens. Area after area of their nature is overtaken, thawed, subjugated, sanctified. Their manners soften. Their words become more gentle. Their conduct more unselfish. As swallows who have found a summer, as frozen buds the spring, their starved humanity bursts into a fuller life. They do not know how it is, but they are different men.

One day they find themselves like their master, going about and doing good. They don't understand their change, but they cannot do otherwise. They were not told to do it; it came to them to do it. But the people who watch them know how to account for it. "They have been," they whisper, "with Jesus." Already the mark and the seal of his character is on them.

"They have been with Jesus." Unparalleled phenomenon, that these poor fishermen should remind other men of Christ! Stupendous victory and mystery of regeneration that mortal men should suggest God to the world!

There is something almost melting in the way his contempo-raries, and John especially, speak of the influence of Christ. John himself lived in daily wonder at Jesus; he was overpowered, over-awed, entranced, transfigured.

To his mind it was impossible for anyone to come under this influence and ever be the same again. No one who abides in him, sins, he said. It was inconceivable that he should sin, as inconceivable as that ice should live in a burning sun, or darkness coexist with noonday. If anyone did sin, it was to John the simple proof that he could never have met Christ. No one who sins, he exclaims, has seen him or knows him.

Friendship

These were Christ's contemporaries. It was easy for them to be influenced by him. They were with him continually. But how can we mirror that which we have never seen? How can these stupendous results be produced by a memory, by the scantiest of all biographies, by one who lived and left this earth two thousand years ago? How can modern men today make Christ, the absent Christ, their most constant companion still? The answer is that friendship is a spiritual thing. It is independent of matter, or space, or time. What I love in my friend is not what I see. What influences me in my friend is not his body but his spirit.

It would have been an awesome experience to have lived at that time. And yet, if Christ were to come into the world again few of us probably would ever have a chance of seeing him. Millions of his subjects would never get within speaking distance of him if he were here. Our companionship with him, like all true companionship, is spiritual communion. All friendship, all love, human and divine, is purely spiritual.

It was after he arose that he most influenced even the disciples. Hence, in reflecting the character of Christ, it is no real obstacle that we never saw him in the flesh.

Imitation—No! Reflection—Yes!

Imitation is mechanical, and reflection is organic. The one is occasional, the other habitual. In the one case, man comes to God and imitates him; in the other, God comes to man and imprints him-self on man. It is quite true that there is an imitation of Christ which amounts to reflection; but Paul's term includes all that the other holds, and is open to no mistake.

"Make Christ your most constant companion" is what this means for us in practical terms. Be more under his influence than under any other influence. Ten minutes spent in his company every day, even two minutes if it were face to face, and heart to heart, will make the whole day different. Every character has an inward spring, let Christ be your spring. Every action has a keynote, let Christ set yours.

Yesterday you got a critical letter. You sat down and wrote a scorching reply. Without a twinge of conscience, you used the cruelest, most cutting adjectives you knew. You did that because your life was set in the wrong key. You began the day with the mirror placed at the wrong angle. Tomorrow, first thing, spend time with him, and your countenance will look different even to your enemy. No matter what you do during this time with him, you'll find you could not write such a letter. Your first impulse may be the same, your judgment may be unchanged; but throughout the whole day your actions, down to the last detail, will reflect that early beginning with him.

Yesterday you thought mostly about yourself, unaware of those around you. Today the poor in spirit will meet you, and you will feed them. The helpless, the tempted, the sad, will crowd around close to you, and you will befriend each one. Where were all these people yesterday? Where they are today, but you did not see them.

In reflected light, the down and out are seen, but your soul today is not at the ordinary angle. "Things which are not seen" are visible. For a few short hours you live the eternal life. The eternal life, the life of faith, is simply the life of the higher vision. Faith is an attitude—a mirror set at the right angle.

When tomorrow is over, and you review it in the evening, you will wonder how you did it. You will not be conscious that you strove for anything, or imitated anything, or crucified anything. You will be conscious of Christ; that he was with you, that without compulsion you were yet compelled, that without force, or noise, or proclamation, the revolution was accomplished.

You do not congratulate yourself as one who has done a mighty deed, or achieved a personal success, or stored up a fund of "Christian experience" to ensure the same result again. You are conscious only of "the glory of the Lord." Those watching you are aware of "the glory of the Lord." In looking at a mirror one does not see the mirror, or think of it, but only of what it reflects. A mirror never calls attention to itself—only when there are flaws in it.

Part Four—*The First Experiment*

Am I reducing religion to a common friendship? No, I'm not talking about a common friendship. There is no such thing in the world. No word on earth is greater or more excellent than friendship. Friendship is the nearest thing we know to what Christianity really is. God is love. And to associate Christianity with friendship is simply to give it the highest expression conceivable by man. Mistakenly, we think some unusual secret lies behind sanctification, some occult experience which only the initiated know.

Thwarted Hopes and Why

Thousands go to church every Sunday hoping to solve this mystery. At meetings, at conferences, many times they have reached what they thought was the very brink of it, but somehow no further revelation came. Poring over religious books, how often they have thought they were within a paragraph of it; the next page, the next sentence, would discover all, and they would be swept along on a flowing tide forever. But nothing happened. The next sentence and the next page were read, and still it eluded them; and though the promise of its coming seemed to be kept faithfully up to the end, the last chapter found them still pursuing.

Why did nothing happen? Because there was nothing to happen; nothing of the kind they were looking for. Why did it elude them? Because there was no "it." We must learn that the pursuit of holiness is simply the pursuit of Christ. Instead of seeking the "it" of a fictitious goal, let's approach a living friend. Sanctity is in character and not in moods; Divinity is in our own plain calm humanity, and not in mystic rapture of the soul.

Mysticism? No!

Some object to a religion expressed in terms of friendship as too mystical. To "abide" in Christ, to "make Christ our most constant companion" is to them the purest mysticism. They want something absolutely tangible and absolutely direct. These people are not looking for signs and wonders but wanting mathematical definition in details. Perhaps it is not possible to reduce this problem to such rigid elements.

The beauty of friendship is its infinity, its boundless limits. We can never drain life of mysticism. Home is full of it, love is full of it, Christianity is full of it. Why do we stumble at this in the relation of man to Christ? It is natural in the relation of man to man.

Perhaps a plain analogy from ordinary life will help us understand this mystical relationship with Christ. How do we know anyone? By communing with their words and thoughts. Many know Dante better than their own fathers. He influences them more. As a spiritual presence he is nearer to them, as a spiritual force more real.

Is there any reason why a greater than Shakespeare or Dante, who walked this earth, who left great words behind him, who has great works everywhere in the world now, should not also instruct, inspire, and mold the characters of men? I do not limit Christ's influence to this. It is this, and more. But Christ, far from resenting or discouraging this relation of friendship, himself proposed it. "Abide in me" was almost his last word to the world. And he partly met the difficulty of those who feel its intangibleness by adding the practical clause, "If ye abide in me, my words abide in you."

Where to Begin

Begin with his words. Usually words do not remain impersonal for long. Christ himself was a word, a word made flesh. Make his words flesh; do them, live them, and you will live Christ. Jesus said: "He that keepeth my commandments, he it is that loveth Me." Obey him and you will love him. Abide in him and you will obey him. Cultivate his friendship. Live after Christ, in his Spirit, as in his presence, and it is difficult to think what more you can do. Take this at least as a first lesson, as introduction.

If you can't instantly and always feel the play of his life on yours, look for it indirectly. "The whole earth is full of the character of the Lord." Christ is the light of the world, and much of his light is reflected from things in the world—even from clouds.

Sunlight is stored in every leaf. The leaf becomes coal, then comforts us when days are dark and we cannot see the sun. Christ shines through men, through books, through history, through nature, music, art. Look for him there. Every day look at the beautiful picture, or hear beautiful music, or read a beautiful poem.

It Takes Time

Do not think work is at a standstill because you do not see yourself grow, or hear the whirr of the machinery. All great things grow noiselessly. You can see a mushroom grow, but never a child. Paul knew this and put it into the heart of his formula. To comfort all slowly perfecting souls he said that they grew "from character to character." "The inward man," he says elsewhere, "is renewed from day to day."

All thorough work is slow; all true development takes place so gradually our senses do not detect any slight changing. The higher the structure, moreover, the slower the progress. As the biologist runs his eye over the long ascent of life he sees the lowest forms of animals develop in an hour; the next above these reach maturity in a day; those higher still take weeks or months to perfect; but the few at the top demand the long experiment of years. If a child and an ape are born on the same day the ape will be in full possession of its faculties and doing the active work of life before the child has left its cradle.

As the man is to the animal in the slowness of his maturation, so the spiritual man is to the natural man. Foundations which have to bear the weight of an eternal life must be surely laid.

Character is to wear forever; who will wonder or grudge that it cannot be developed in a day? To await the growing of a soul, nevertheless, is an almost divine act of faith. One can understand the impatience of deformity with itself, of a consciously despicable character standing before Christ, wondering, yearning, hungering to be like him. Yet one must trust the process fearlessly, and without misgiving. "The Lord, the Spirit" will do his part.

Desiring instant or visible progress, we are tempted to hurry. We try less spiritual methods, or defeat the end by watching for effects instead of keeping our eyes on the cause.

The creation of a new heart, the renewing of a right spirit, is an omnipotent work of God. Leave it to the Creator. "For I am confident of this very thing, that He who began a good work in you will perfect it until the day of Christ Jesus" (Phil. 1:6).

However, no man who feels the value and importance of what is at stake will be careless with his progress. To become like Christ is the only thing in the world worth caring for. All other ambitions of man are foolish and all lesser achievements empty. Only those who make this pursuit the supreme desire and passion of their lives can even begin to hope to reach it.

Passivity?

It may have seemed up to this point as if all depended on passivity. Let me now assert, with intense conviction, that all depends on activity. A religion of effortless adoration may be a religion for an angel but never for a man. Not in the contemplative but in the active lies true hope; not in rapture but in reality lies true life; not in the realm of ideals but among tangible things is man's sanctification brought about.

Resolution, effort, pain, self-crucifixion, agony—all the things already dismissed as futile in themselves must now be restored to office, and a tenfold responsibility laid on them. What is their job? It is to move the vast inertia of the soul, to place it, and keep it where the spiritual forces will act on it. It is to rally the forces of the will, and keep the surface of the mirror bright, always in position. It is to direct our gaze, our attention to Christ, and away from the influence and pull of the world.

To photograph the spectrum of a star long ago an astronomer entered his darkened observatory with a lighted candle. Did he light the candle so he could see the star? No. He needed light to adjust the instruments. The star would make the photograph, but the astronomer also had responsibilities. For a long time he worked in the dimness, screwing tubes and polishing lenses and adjusting reflectors, and only after much labor the finely focused instrument was brought in line. Then he blew out the light, and left the star alone to do its work on the plate.

The day's task for the Christian is to bring his instrument in line. Having done that he may blow out his candle.

All the evidences of Christianity
   which have brought him there,
all aids to faith,
all acts of worship,
all the leverages of the church,
all prayer and meditation,
all girding of the will—
   these lesser processes,
   these candlelight activities for that supreme hour
   may be set aside but for an hour.

The wise man will quickly relight his candle; the wisest man will never let it go out. Tomorrow, or the next moment, he may need it again to focus the image better, to take a speck off the lens, or to clear the mirror from the dulling breath of the world.

Readjustment to Follow Christ

The star needs no readjustment. Christ is the one great fixed point in this shifting universe. The world moves. And each day, each hour, demands a further motion and readjustment for the soul. A telescope in an observatory follows a star like clockwork, but the clockwork of the soul is called the will. The soul passively reflects the image of the Lord, while the will actively holds the mirror in position. Why this deliberate effort? Because the drifting and pulling motion of the world can take the soul out of alignment.

To follow Christ is to keep the soul in position to allow for the motion of the earth. This deliberate holding of the inner man exactly opposite Jesus, accurately steadies him through all the storms and conflicts of life. This is the stupendous cooperating labor of the will. It is all man's work. It is all Christ's work. In practice, it is both; in theory it is both. But the wise man will say, "It depends on me."

A famous statue stands in the Galerie des Beaux Arts in Paris. It was the last work of a great genius. Very poor, he lived in a garret, which served as a combined studio and sleeping-room. When the statue was almost finished, one midnight a sudden frost fell on Paris. The sculptor lay awake in the fireless room and thought of the still moist clay, thought how the water would freeze in the pores and destroy in an hour the dream of his life. So the old man rose from his couch and heaped the bedclothes reverently round his work. In the morning when the neighbors entered the room the sculptor was dead. But the statue was protected from the cold.

The image of Christ that is forming within us—that is life's one goal. Let every project stand aside for that. "Till Christ be formed" no man's work is finished, and no life has fulfilled its end. Has the work begun? When, and how are we to be different? Time cannot change men. Death cannot change men. Christ can. Therefore, put on Christ.

Conclusion

There is a good possibility that at this juncture you may be asking one of these questions.

How can I be sure this is the way?
How can I practically go about taking this way?
Is this really scripturally based, or is it just another misuse of proof text?

Perhaps your spirit bears witness with the truth of this message. Or you may be saying, "Yes, this is right." No matter where you are in your quest, I hope you are interested in how this can become a reality in your life.

To confirm the truth of this message in your heart and help you get a handle on how to work this out in your life, I am including a Scripture list that you can use to confirm, through the help of the Spirit, that this teaching is New Testament, and part of the glorious gospel. I hope you will read them prayerfully.

May our Lord lead you to himself and to the simplicity of Christian growth and life. May you find to be true what Augustine said years ago. "You made us for yourself and we never rest until we rest in thee."

Scripture

From the Gospels	*From the New Testament Letters*
Mark 12:28–31	Romans 8 and 12:1–2
Luke 10:38–42	2 Corinthians 3
John 6:26–64	2 Corinthians 4:16; 5:21
John 5:17–36	Galatians 3:1–3, 23; 4:11; 5:1–26
John 14:9–27	Ephesians 1:11–23; 2:19-22; 3:14–21
John 15:1–27	Colossians 1:9–2:3
John 16:1–15	Hebrews 8:6–13; 10:19-24; 12:14–29
	1 Peter 2:2–5
	2 Peter 1:1–8
	1 John 4:7–8